LIFE ISSUES, MEDICAL CHOICES

Life Issues, Medical Choices

QUESTIONS AND ANSWERS FOR CATHOLICS

Janet E. Smith and Christopher Kaczor

PUBLISHED BY ST. ANTHONY MESSENGER PRESS
CINCINNATI, OHIO

LIBRARY OF CONGRESS CATALOGING-IN-PUBLICATION DATA

Smith, Janet E.
  Life issues, medical choices : questions and answers for Catholics /
Janet E. Smith and Christopher Kaczor.
        p. cm.
  Includes bibliographical references.
  ISBN 978-0-86716-808-2 (pbk. : alk. paper) 1. Medical ethics—
Religious aspects—Catholic Church—Miscellanea. 2. Life and death,
Power over—
Religious aspects—Catholic Church—Miscellanea. 3. Human reproduc-
tive technology—Religious aspects—Catholic Church—Miscellanea. 4.
Contraception—Religious aspects—Catholic Church—Miscellanea. 5.
Euthanasia—Religious aspects—Catholic Church—Miscellanea. 6.
Christian ethics—Catholic authors—Miscellanea. 7. Catholic Church—
Doctrines. I. Kaczor, Christopher Robert, 1969- II. Title.

R725.56.S62 2007
174.2—dc22

2007022141

ISBN 978-0-86716-808-2

Published by Servant Books, an imprint of
St. Anthony Messenger Press
28 W. Liberty St.
Cincinnati, OH 45202
www.ServantBooks.org

Printed in the United States of America.
Printed on acid-free paper.

07 08 09 10 11 5 4 3 2 1

Contents

INTRODUCTION / xiii

CHAPTER ONE: **Fundamentals**

Question 1: From a philosophical perspective, what is the value of human life? / 1

Question 2: Why do Catholics value human life so highly? / 4

Question 3: What is the meaning of suffering from a Christian perspective? / 8

Question 4: What does it mean to say that Catholics must follow their consciences? / 15

Question 5: Are Catholics always obliged to follow Church teaching? / 18

Question 6: If a Catholic in ignorance of Church teaching does something contrary to that teaching, such as using in vitro fertilization, does he or she sin? / 22

Question 7: What kinds of actions are intrinsically evil? / 25

Question 8: What does it mean to say that an action is a matter of "prudential judgment"? / 27

Question 9: What is the principle of double effect? / 28

CHAPTER TWO: **Beginning-of-Life Issues**

Question 10: Why is abortion wrong? / 33

Question 11: Since an early embryo can split into twins, is an embryo really an individual? Before the brain develops, is an embryo really rational? / 40

Question 12: Since an embryo cannot experience pain until several weeks into the pregnancy, would abortion be moral before that time? / 43

Question 13: Would abortion to relieve the mental distress of a pregnant woman be moral? / 45

Question 14: Is it moral to have an abortion if the unborn child is handicapped? / 46

Question 15: Is it immoral to use "excess" embryos for research? / 48

Question 16: Which ways of treating ectopic pregnancies are moral? / 52

Question 17: Is it ever morally permissible to induce labor prematurely? / 56

CHAPTER THREE: **Reproductive Technologies**

Question 18: Which reproductive technologies are moral? / 60

Question 19: Is cloning wrong? / 65

Question 20: Is it moral to have a baby in order to provide for the medical needs of an already existing child? / 66

Question 21: Is it morally permissible to "adopt" a frozen embryo? / 68

Question 22: Is it moral to attempt to have a child when genetic factors make it likely that the child may be mentally or physically handicapped? / 69

Question 23: Is it moral to try to select the sex of one's baby? / 70

Question 24: Are ovarian transplants morally permissible? / 72

CHAPTER FOUR: **Contraception, Sterilization and Natural Family Planning**

Question 25: Why does the Church teach that contraception is intrinsically immoral? / 74

Question 26: Isn't Natural Family Planning just another form of contraception? / 80

Question 27: If contraception is intrinsically evil, why does the Church permit women to take contraceptives for medical purposes? / 83

Question 28: Is it moral for spouses to use a condom if one of them has the human immunodeficiency virus (HIV)? / 86

Question 29: Is it morally permissible to have sex with a contracepting spouse? / 88

Question 30: Is it moral to use contraceptives as post-rape treatment? / 90

Question 31: Should parents have their daughters receive the vaccine for the human papillomavirus (HPV)? / 91

Question 32: Would it be moral to put a mentally handicapped woman on a contraceptive or have her sterilized if she is at risk of being sexually abused? / 92

Question 33: Is it morally permissible for a woman to be sterilized if her uterus is so damaged that she could not get through a pregnancy safely? / 94

Question 34: Are couples who have been sterilized morally obliged to get a reversal? / 95

CHAPTER FIVE: **End-of-Life Issues**

Question 35: What is euthanasia? / 98

Question 36: Is there an ethical difference between *active* euthanasia (intending the death of the patient by some act) and *passive* euthanasia (intending the death of the patient by some omission)? / 100

Question 37: Is it always wrong to let someone die? / 101

Question 38: Is life always a good, even when it involves great suffering? / 102

Question 39: What is the Christian view of the relationship of the soul to the body, and how does it influence the moral evaluation of end-of-life treatments? / 105

Question 40: What is the difference between ordinary means and extraordinary means of preserving life? / 109

Question 41: Should food and water be provided for patients in a persistent vegetative state? / 112

Question 42: How should one respond to the request "Will you help me die?" / 115

Question 43: Are advance directives helpful? / 118

Question 44: Why does the determination of death matter? / 120

Question 45: What is "brain death"? Does the Church approve of using neurological criteria to determine death? / 121

Question 46: What is the "non-heart-beating donor" procedure for obtaining organs? Is it morally acceptable? / 126

Question 47: Do hospital futility policies accord with Catholic morality? / 128

Question 48: What is the sacrament of the sick? When should Catholics have recourse to it? / 130

CHAPTER SIX: **Cooperation With Evil**

Question 49: Sometimes health care professionals are asked to perform actions that may make them guilty of cooperating with the evil actions of others, such as assisting in abortion. How do these workers know when they must refuse to do certain things? / 133

Question 50: Is it moral for a Catholic pharmacist to fill prescriptions for contraceptives? Is it moral for a Catholic nurse to give Depo-Provera shots? / 136

Question 51: What is scandal? In the practice of medicine, what kind of behavior causes scandal? / 139

Question 52: Is it moral to use vaccines that have been produced from aborted fetuses? / 141

Question 53: Is it morally acceptable to separate conjoined twins? / 144

Question 54: Is it moral to have a healthy breast removed because of a genetic propensity to breast cancer? / 147

Question 55: What if a patient cannot be persuaded to do what is morally correct? / 148

Question 56: Does a physician need to respect the decision of a Jehovah's Witness to refuse a blood transfusion? / 153

Question 57: What steps should a Catholic working at a Catholic hospital take in the face of evidence that the hospital or those working there are engaging in practices recognized by the Church as incompatible with true human dignity? / 156

CHAPTER SEVEN: **The Ten Commandments for Health Care Professionals and Patients** / 160

HELPFUL RESOURCES / 172

NOTES / 179

INDEX / 189

Introduction

The primary source of truth for Catholics is Jesus Christ. He is the fullness of truth and the teacher of the truth. He is the foundation of our faith and should guide our actions and intentions.

But the slogan "What would Jesus do?" does not provide all the guidance that decision makers need about complex bioethical issues. Yes, Jesus always did the loving thing, and that is what we should do, too, but it is not always easy to determine what the loving thing is. Is it loving to provide artificial nutrition and hydration to a patient in a persistent vegetative state, or is it loving to withdraw it and allow the patient to die? Is it loving to use human embryos to try to find a cure for Alzheimer's?

Fortunately, Christ teaches not only through his words and actions but also through the gift of reason and through the Church. While Catholics depend upon the explicit teachings of Christ as recorded in Scripture and the guidance of the Holy Spirit, we also use our reason to discover natural truth and the full meaning of the theological truths relevant to ethics.

The Catholic Church has immense respect for the power of human beings to discover truth simply through experiencing reality and thinking carefully about it. God gave us our ability to think to enable us to discover truth. Thus the Church has fostered intellectual inquiry of every kind:

philosophical, scientific, artistic, as well as theological. Indeed, the first universities were Catholic, and they were marked by a lively interest in all facets of human life.

Throughout the Church's intellectual history, Catholic theologians and philosophers have made major contributions to medical ethics, both in its modern form as a specialized discipline and historically as a set of issues in ethics and moral theology. The Vatican has pontifical academies and councils dedicated to the sciences, the arts and life issues, and it regularly sponsors international conferences on various bioethical issues. Catholic health care workers have established professional organizations to advance their understanding of Catholic moral issues.

Given this understanding of reason, it comes as no surprise that pre-Christian philosophers affirm many ethical principles that the Church embraces. The proper relationship of the physician to the patient has been a concern of philosophy from the start. The Hippocratic Oath (from the fifth century BC) is one of the earliest expressions of medical ethics, and for millennia physicians took the oath as a way of proclaiming their intention to practice medicine morally. It is important to note that the oath disallowed both abortion and euthanasia.

Fundamental Christian truths, such as the concept of human dignity and the meaning of human suffering, illuminate and deepen what our reason can discover and are invaluable guideposts for understanding reality, as well as for formulating bioethical principles. Concerned that we live fully moral lives, the Church has developed a tradition of reasoning which includes both the natural law tradition and theological reflection based on revelation. By means of this reasoning, it has articulated fundamental principles to guide our thinking about moral issues and also applied those principles to issues that touch our daily lives. Catholic thinkers have developed some of the most fundamental principles of bioethics, such as the principle of double effect and the principle of cooperation with evil.

The Challenge Today

Pope John Paul II asked Catholics to establish a "civilization of love." He exhorted us not to be afraid to proclaim the truth and to be heroic in our witness to truth and in our loving service of others. Those in the health care professions are uniquely situated both to provide loving service and to give witness to the truth.

In *Evangelium Vitae* ("Gospel of Life"), Pope John Paul II's encyclical dedicated to the life issues, he speaks about a conflict between the culture of life and the culture of death. He bemoans the fact that the culture of death has infiltrated the medical profession, a profession that by its very nature is directed to protecting life. He notes that attacks against life

> tend no longer to be considered as 'crimes'; paradoxically they assume the nature of 'rights,' to the point that the State is called upon to give them legal recognition and to make them available through the free services of health-care personnel. Such attacks strike human life at the time of its greatest frailty, when it lacks any means of self-defence." (11)

Catholics desperately need Catholic health care professionals to be true to their profession and their faith, so that a reverence for life can again permeate the health care profession and the larger culture as well.

Not only has the attack on life infiltrated the health care profession, it has infiltrated the home. In *Evangelium Vitae* Pope John Paul II goes on to say: "Even more serious is the fact that, most often, those attacks are carried out in the very heart of and with the complicity of the family—the family which by its nature is called to be the 'sanctuary of life'" (11). Families often comply with such practices as abortion, in vitro fertilization and assisted suicide.

We live in a culture permeated by a moral relativism that often mistakes license for true freedom and that generally has become skeptical about the possibility of any certain knowledge, especially in the realm of morality. Unfortunately, many Catholics have been shaped more by this relativist, secular culture than by a faith that begins with a radical love for Jesus Christ and is nurtured by the Church he established.

Catholics demonstrate their love for Christ and his Church by using the gifts of their intellects to learn what the Church teaches about the challenging issues of our time and attempting to live out that teaching in their free decisions. True freedom lies in the ability to align one's actions freely with the truth, so as to achieve authentic human happiness both now and in the life to come. Jesus promised, "If you continue in my word, you are truly my disciples, and you will know the truth, and the truth will make you free" (John 8:31–32).

Some Questions and Answers

This book is an effort both to provide a basic presentation of the fundamental principles of Catholic thought and to explain how to apply these principles to specific issues.

Some principles and questions require a fairly extensive discussion, whereas others we can explain quite expeditiously once the fundamental principles are understood. We hope to help fellow Catholics understand and embrace the sometimes difficult teachings of the Church on medical and moral matters. Nearly every Catholic will face difficult decisions about medical treatment, either with their own health or in the care of loved ones.

We have divided the subject matter into eight parts. The first chapter establishes some of the most fundamental principles that undergird the Church's teaching on bioethics, including information on the different levels of Church teaching and the question of freedom of conscience.

The second chapter takes up questions on life in the womb. Most Catholics accept the Church's teaching on abortion; you will find here a thorough treatment of the topic that is intended to put to rest any remaining doubts and enable you to be effective partners in discourse with others. The discussion on embryonic research bears upon some pressing issues of our times.

The third chapter treats the very controversial issues of reproductive technologies, such as in vitro fertilization. Many Catholics have a difficult time with the Church's teachings on these issues. If life is such a great good, why does the Church condemn some of the means that help the infertile conceive?

The fourth chapter deals with another challenging area for Catholics: birth control. Here too we apply fundamental principles to explain why the Church opposes contraception and sterilization yet supports Natural Family Planning.

The fifth chapter gives some valuable guidelines for making decisions about end-of-life issues that are faithful to Church teaching.

The sixth chapter takes up a myriad of issues that relate in some way to the question of cooperation with evil. The Church teaches that we may never do evil directly, but health care workers must often use procedures that do harm as well as good. The principles we present in this chapter can help Catholics determine when permitting some bad consequences is morally acceptable.

In the seventh chapter we apply the Ten Commandments to the actions of health care professionals and patients as well. A final section provides a short list of helpful supplementary resources.

Pope John Paul II's encyclical letter The Splendor of Truth (*Veritatis splendor*) states: "No one can escape from the fundamental questions: *What must I do? How do I distinguish good from evil?*" (2). These questions are often precisely the questions that trouble Catholics facing medical choices. For all the clarity and depth of its understanding on bioethical issues, the Church has not answered all questions that face us. In this age of rapid technological and medical advance, new issues regularly arise, requiring careful assessment by moral theologians. Eventually the Church may address some of these unsettled issues explicitly; this book provides guidance on how to make decisions in light of the principles articulated by the Church thus far.

It is also the case that ethical decisions involve many factual details pertinent to specific situations. While clarity may exist on the level of general truths, applying these general truths to a particular situation is the task of those thoroughly familiar with the facts of that situation. The authors of this book hope that our presentation of the general truths about bioethical issues will guide individuals in the particular decisions they face.

CHAPTER ONE

Fundamentals

Question 1: From a philosophical perspective, what is the value of human life?

Catholics believe that the truth about the value of life comes to us not only through revelation but also through natural law. We believe, for instance, that God has "written on our hearts" that it is wrong to kill an innocent human being. The laws of virtually all nations, until very recently, reflected the nearly universal belief that no one should kill innocent human life intentionally. Philosophers such as Plato and Kant argued that killing an innocent human being—including oneself—is morally wrong.

Philosophers distinguish three different views about the value of human life: (1) life has *absolute* value, and everything possible must be done to keep people alive; (2) only lives of a certain *quality* should be preserved; (3) human life is *sacred*, and we must honor its sacredness, but we also must not be afraid of death as if it were the worst possible evil. The Church and many philosophers embrace this third view.

The first view—that life is an *absolute* value—holds that not only is it wrong to kill innocent human beings intentionally but also every effort must be made to preserve and extend the duration of human life, regardless of circumstances. According to this view, not only would it be wrong to do anything to end or shorten human life, but it also would be wrong to fail to provide any treatment that would prolong life. No expense or effort should be spared, the thought goes, even for those for whom death is imminent or those who are receiving very little benefit from various treatments.

This is not the teaching of the Church. *Evangelium Vitae* states:

> Euthanasia must be distinguished from the decision to forego so-called "aggressive medical treatment," in other words, medical procedures which no longer correspond to the real situation of the patient, either because they are by now disproportionate to any expected results or because they impose an excessive burden on the patient and his family. In such situations, when death is clearly imminent and inevitable, one can in conscience "refuse forms of treatment that would only secure a precarious and burdensome prolongation of life, so long as the normal care due to the sick person in similar cases is not interrupted." (65)[1]

The Church teaches that we certainly have an obligation to care for our health, to seek treatment for diseases and ailments and to seek to prolong our lives, but it also teaches that "to forego extraordinary or disproportionate means is not the equivalent of suicide or euthanasia; it rather expresses acceptance of the human condition in the face of death" (*Evangelium Vitae*, 65). (See question 40 on the differences between ordinary and extraordinary treatment.)

Those who hold the second view of the value of human life—that only lives of a certain quality have value—believe it moral sometimes to end lives considered no longer worth living. That is, this view holds that those who have a good *quality* of life have lives worth preserving, whereas those whose quality of life is bad—who are suffering a great deal or who no longer can take part in activities that once made life enjoyable—could morally do something to end their lives. *Evangelium Vitae* speaks about this view:

> We are faced with one of the more alarming symptoms of the "culture of death," which is advancing above all in prosperous societies, marked by an attitude of excessive preoccupation with efficiency and which sees the growing number of elderly and disabled people as intolerable and too burdensome. These people are very often isolated by their families and by society, which are organized almost exclusively on the basis of criteria of productive efficiency, according to which a hopelessly impaired life no longer has any value. (64)

The Christian is to respond to those who have a life "hopelessly impaired" as a beautiful opportunity to demonstrate, by the care and attention they give to the impaired, that those suffering impairment very much remain in God's love.

Evangelium Vitae maintains that the modern age has come to value "having" over "being":

> The values of *being* are replaced by those of *having*. The only goal which counts is the pursuit of one's own material well-being. The so-called "quality of life" is interpreted primarily or exclusively as economic efficiency, inordinate consumerism, physical beauty and pleasure, to the neglect of the more profound dimensions—interpersonal, spiritual and religious—of existence. (23)

The value of "being" means that simply to exist as a human being is of great value since all human beings are ordered to goodness, beauty and truth, even when they are

3

greatly incapacitated and unable to realize this great potential. Even human beings who seem no longer to have any cognitive abilities or abilities to respond to the external world live in relationships to other human beings, and as *Evangelium Vitae* states, they "communicate through the silent language of a profound sharing of affection" (19).

Although life is intrinsically valuable, death is not something that should be avoided at all costs. For instance, sometimes we are called to sacrifice our lives for a noble cause, as when a hero falls upon a hand grenade to save his comrades or a martyr dies for the faith. Indeed, we must remember that Christians understand death to be a door to eternal happiness: Those who die in a state of grace transition to heaven, a place of everlasting joy. Thus, sustaining life as long as possible should not be our goal, but rather our goal should be to love God and neighbor throughout our earthly lives and so prepare for eternal life.

Question 2: Why do Catholics value human life so highly?

To answer this question we look both to Scripture and to the Magisterium.

Scriptural Teaching

While even those who do not believe in God are capable of recognizing that human life has intrinsic value, those who believe in God, and especially those who are Christians, have special reason to value life. After all, "God is love" (1 John 4:16), and he created the whole universe out of love. God made human beings to receive his love, to return his love and to give love to others. Human beings were not made for some "useful purpose": we are what philosophers call "ends in ourselves." We have no other ultimate purpose than to live eternally with God.

It is an astonishing truth that God made human beings in his image. An immortal, rational, free and loving God made beings who have immortal souls and who are rational, free and made to love and to be loved. Human life is sacred because it specifically reflects the nature of the divine.

Scripture tells a story of human existence that explains both why human beings are of such great value and why we struggle so much. God entered into a covenant relationship of unconditional love with human beings; this was broken by original sin. In the process human beings injured their relationship with each other and caused great disturbances or disorder in their souls. God promised even after this break—what we call "the Fall"—that he would remain faithful to his love and would send a savior to rescue human beings from sin and alienation.

This relationship between God and human beings continues throughout the course of salvation history. Abraham, Isaac, Jacob, David, Moses and all the prophets point to a resounding truth: God loves and exercises providential care for each and every human being, particularly those who suffer—for instance, the poor, the persecuted, the diseased, the forgotten, the unwanted. He also cares for all sinners, even terrible sinners—such as murderers, adulterers and idolaters. God cares for the human family as a whole and for each one of us individually.

For Christians, Jesus Christ—truly God and truly man— exemplifies the unique value of each human person, for God became man to show the love of the Father for each of us. The Incarnation, the fact that God was willing to unite himself with human nature, itself points to the dignity of human nature. Each stage of human life—from conception, gestation, birth, growth, maturity and even to death itself—was made holy by the God-man.

Not only the Incarnation of Jesus but also his teachings and actions reflect the value of each human being. "As you did it to one of the least of these my brethren, you did it to me," Jesus said (Matthew 25:40). Jesus commands us to feed the hungry, clothe the naked, comfort the distressed, free captives and teach those lacking knowledge. Wherever there is a human need, there is a chance to serve the Lord in disguise.

As if to underscore the fact that not just some people but all people merit respect, Jesus repeatedly reached out to people on the margins of society. He offered his healing touch to the diseased, including lepers, fed the hungry and even raised the dead to new life.

Magisterial Teaching

Not only revelation and reason but also the magisterium of the Church has made known to Catholics the truth about the value of human life. This teaching of the Catholic Church could not be clearer. Pope John Paul II stated strongly that life at all its stages is sacred and worthy of protection:

> By the authority which Christ conferred upon Peter and his Successors, and in communion with the Bishops of the Catholic Church, I confirm that the direct and voluntary killing of an innocent human being is always gravely immoral. This doctrine, based upon that unwritten law which man, in

the light of reason, finds in his own heart (cf. Rom 2:14–15), is reaffirmed by Sacred Scripture, transmitted by the Tradition of the Church and taught by the ordinary and universal Magisterium.

The deliberate decision to deprive an innocent human being of his life is always morally evil and can never be licit either as an end in itself or as a means to a good end. It is in fact a grave act of disobedience to the moral law, and indeed to God himself, the author and guarantor of that law; it contradicts the fundamental virtues of justice and charity. "Nothing and no one can in any way permit the killing of an innocent human being, whether a fetus or an embryo, an infant or an adult, an old person, or one suffering from an incurable disease, or a person who is dying. Furthermore, no one is permitted to ask for this act of killing, either for himself or herself or for another person entrusted to his or her care, nor can he or she consent to it, either explicitly or implicitly. Nor can any authority legitimately recommend or permit such an action." (*Evangelium Vitae*, 57)[2]

The language of this passage makes it very clear that this teaching is authoritative, and indeed it has the marks of an infallible teaching, as articulated by Vatican II (see *Lumen Gentium,* 25). The Holy Father invokes his authority as Vicar of Christ on earth. He makes reference to all the sources of truth Catholics have to draw upon: natural law, Scripture, the Magisterium.

John Paul II makes it clear that we cannot kill innocent human beings, especially the particularly vulnerable in our time: the unborn, the aged, the dying, those who suffer chronically. We may not ask others to kill us, nor may the state advocate or allow such actions. Catholics, given our understanding that we are all creatures made by a loving

God for an eternal union with him, have special reason to promote, protect and defend the lives of all human beings.

Question 3: What is the meaning of suffering from a Christian perspective?

Bioethical questions and medical decisions are often related to the question of suffering. Medical treatments seek to relieve suffering, but sometimes they also cause it or allow it to continue. Our discussion of bioethics would be incomplete if it did not address, however briefly and incompletely, the problem of suffering.

Since our understanding of God remains fragile and incomplete, we have no hope of providing a definitive treatment of suffering here, especially since we are dealing with suffering in its subjective dimension—as experienced by the one who currently is suffering. Like the multi-dimensional experience of love, the experience of suffering is complex. Thus to offer a simple solution to suffering does not do justice to the complexities of the topic. Words simply cannot express adequately the offensiveness of suffering nor provide a simple solution for the problem of pain.

The Meaning of Suffering
Pope John Paul II knew about human suffering from personal experience and also possessed great wisdom, both natural and supernatural, so it is fitting that we draw on his insights to handle this profound question. Despite the personal pain he suffered in various ways throughout his life, John Paul was a man filled to overflowing with joy. He had found an answer to the problem of suffering, and that answer is Christ.

John Paul experienced the *mystery* of suffering—the affliction endured to a greater or lesser extent by every single human person—but he also knew the *meaning* of suffering. He explored this in his Apostolic Letter on the Christian Meaning of Human Suffering (*Salvifici Doloris*).[3]

Every human person suffers in a variety of ways: physically, psychologically, socially and spiritually. Indeed, suffering is linked to the very existence of the human person, from birth until death. Who does not ask: "Why do I suffer? Why do others suffer? How can this suffering be overcome? Is there any meaning to suffering?"

The Bible, Pope John Paul II noted, provides many examples of human suffering, including (but not limited to) one's own death, the danger of death, the death of one's children and friends, sterility, homesickness, persecution, mockery, scorn, loneliness, abandonment, remorse of conscience, the prospering of the wicked and the suffering of the just, unfaithfulness of spouse and friends and the misfortunes of one's own nation (see *Salvifici Doloris*, 6).

What then are the meanings of suffering? In certain situations, an evil—such as suffering—makes possible some important good. Were God to eliminate that evil, the corresponding good would also be eliminated. What are some of those goods?

John Paul II stated that suffering can build character in and display the virtue of the one who suffers: "And if the Lord consents to test Job with suffering, he does it *to demonstrate the latter's righteousness*. The suffering has the nature of a test" (*Salvifici Doloris*, 11). The Holy Father also said that suffering can "unleash love" in those who care for the suffering person (*Salvifici Doloris*, 29). It is the weaknesses of others, the needs of others and the sufferings of others that make possible acts of charity toward them. At times we only discover the depth of how much someone cares for us when we find ourselves in need of care.

Suffering also breaks down that most fundamental of human proclivities, the desire to be God. The atheistic philosopher Jean Paul Sartre wrote: "Man is the being whose project is to be God.... To be man means to reach toward being God. Or if you prefer, man fundamentally is the desire to be God."[4] What is the original sin of Adam and Eve but a reordering of the universe, where human beings have the knowledge of God, where they determine what is good and what is evil? Is not this original sin replicated in some way in each and every human sin? The person who commits sin orders the universe according to his own will, setting aside the will of God.

Redemptive Suffering

Suffering is redemptive in part because it definitively reveals to man that he is not in fact God, and it thereby opens the human person to receive the divine:

> *To suffer* means to become particularly *susceptible,* particularly *open to the working of the salvific powers of God,* offered to humanity in Christ. In him God has confirmed his desire to act especially through suffering, which is man's weakness and emptying of self, and he wishes to make his power known precisely in this weakness and emptying of self." (*Salvifici Doloris,* 23)

Only in human weakness do many of us begin to rely on God and explicitly repudiate our own divine ambitions. Every pain alerts us to the fact that we are not the Almighty.

History provides many examples of sinners transformed into saints on the occasion of suffering, Saint Francis of Assisi and Saint Ignatius of Loyola perhaps most memorably. The French novelist Leon Bloy once said that there is only one tragedy in life: not to be a saint. It may be that God permits some suffering as the only way to wake someone from a dream of self-sufficiency and illusory happiness.

A Result of Sin?

Job's friends were of the impression that all suffering endured by a person is the direct result of that person's sin. They reasoned that since Job was suffering, he must have personally sinned against God. In *Salvifici Doloris* John Paul II uses the story of Job to make precisely the opposite point: *"It is not true that all suffering is a consequence of a fault and has the nature of a punishment"* (11). The innocent do suffer. Frequently bad things happen to good people, and the fact that people suffer is no evidence that they are not really good.

In the New Testament Christ by his passion teaches the same truth. That Jesus suffered greatly is clear from a reading of the Gospels or a viewing of *The Passion of the Christ*. The Lamb of God, who was without sin, suffered at the hands of evil men and also from the abandonment of his friends. Jesus, though entirely without fault, endured rejection, beating, taunting, flogging and crucifixion, not to mention the severe internal suffering he must have felt in contemplating the betrayal of his apostles and the sinfulness of all mankind. Surely the suffering of Jesus removes the moral stigma attached to suffering, for it shows that personal suffering does not indicate personal ethical failure nor God's abandonment.

Indeed, the suffering of Christ overcomes the worst possible suffering of the human person: permanent alienation from God, the source and summit of all goodness. All suffering in this life—like all happiness in this life—is imperfect, partial and finite. Hell, on the other hand, is complete separation from God, and it lasts forever. The worst human suffering on earth pales in comparison to hell's pains. From this most definitive suffering possible, Jesus saves his people.

The cross is the means of overcoming all suffering, the moral suffering of sin and the physical suffering of death. "Precisely *by means of this suffering* he [Jesus] must bring it about 'that man should not perish, but have eternal life.' Precisely by means of his Cross he must strike at the roots of evil, planted in the history of man and in human souls. Precisely by means of his Cross he must accomplish *the work of salvation*" (*Salvifici Doloris*, 16). From the greatest possible evil—a human being entirely without fault and entirely good in every respect, suffering unjustly the greatest possible pain—God brings about the greatest good— the salvation of the human family, a redemption from pain and suffering for those who do not themselves merit this redemption.

Caring for the Suffering

One might be tempted to think that the Christian approach to the problem of suffering is akin to Buddhist resignation in the face of pain. If suffering completes the redemptive work of Christ, then perhaps we should not alleviate suffering, and maybe we should even cause suffering.

However, "Christ's revelation of the salvific meaning of suffering *is in no way identified with an attitude of passivity.*

Completely the reverse is true. The Gospel is the negation of passivity in the face of suffering. Christ himself is especially active in this field" (*Salvifici Doloris*, 30). The works of Christ were to restore sight to the blind, heal the leper and give food to the hungry. He taught that we should love God and neighbor, and he gave us the parable of the Good Samaritan to illustrate the duty of all Christians to look after the needs of others.

In fact, Jesus tells us that our final judgment hinges on our care for suffering people:

> Come, O blessed of my Father, inherit the kingdom prepared for you from the foundation of the world; for I was hungry and you gave me food, I was thirsty and you gave me drink, I was a stranger and you welcomed me, I was naked and you clothed me, I was sick and you visited me, I was in prison and you came to me. (Matthew 25:34–36)

Although it is true that God can bring good, great good, out of suffering, suffering nevertheless is connected with evil (see *Salvifici Doloris*, 7). The fact that good can come from evil and that evil can come from good does not change good into evil or evil into good. The Christian understanding of the meaning of suffering does not beget an indifference to suffering but rather the expression of faith in charitable works, including care for the sick.

Faith and Suffering

Viktor Frankl, in his book *Man's Search for Meaning*, describes his horrifying experiences in Nazi concentration camps. He notes that prisoners in the exact same material circumstances—among the most horrible imaginable—did not all react in the same way. Some prisoners purposely killed themselves by walking into electrified fences; others clung to life and even found joy despite the atrocities daily occurring around them. What made the difference?

One way to put it is that man can endure anything if he has a reason to live, and conversely, man can endure little if he does not have a reason to live. Those who love Christ and seek to imitate him have a reason to live and a motivation to endure suffering. Pope John Paul II stated:

> A source of joy is found in the *overcoming of the sense of the uselessness of suffering,* a feeling that is sometimes very strongly rooted in human suffering. This feeling not only consumes the person interiorly, but seems to make him a burden to others. The person feels condemned to receive help and assistance from others, and at the same time seems useless to himself. The discovery of the salvific meaning of suffering in union with Christ *transforms* this depressing *feeling.* Faith in sharing in the suffering of Christ brings with it the interior certainty that the suffering person "completes what is lacking in Christ's afflictions"; the certainty that in the spiritual dimension of the work of Redemption *he is serving,* like Christ, *the salvation of his brothers and sisters.* Therefore he is carrying out an irreplaceable service. (*Salvifici Doloris,* 27)

Christ gives us a reason to live, however much we suffer, by offering us a share in his life and his love for others. The suffering of Christ thereby redeems suffering itself. Not only does Christ teach through his words and actions that suffering is not necessarily the result of the personal guilt of the one who suffers, but also he opens up the possibility that the one who suffers can share in the redemptive work of Christ (see *Salvifici Doloris,* 19).

The suffering of Christ leads to his glory, and so too the sufferings of Christians for the kingdom of God lead to their glory. Indeed, Paul writes, "Now I rejoice in my sufferings for your sake, and in my flesh I *complete what is lacking in Christ's afflictions* for the sake of his body, that is, the Church" (Colossians 1:24, emphasis added). All of our suffering can be united with and offered to Christ as a prayer for human redemption.

Question 4: What does it mean to say that Catholics must follow their consciences?

The Catholic Church teaches that every person should follow his or her conscience, since the conscience is a person's internal "compass" for what is right or wrong in a particular circumstance. Actions that spring from some source other than conscience are less than fully human. For example, actions done out of whim, pure impulse, fear or unthinking habit do not reflect fully the human person's ability to think about reality and to have his or her best judgments govern his or her choices.

Fully human behavior flows from the ability to choose in accord with the truth that one knows. The dignity of the human person is rooted in the conscience and the freedom of the will. That is, human beings, unlike other earthly creatures, have the freedom to make decisions that have a moral dimension. These decisions shape the person's character for good or evil and impact the world.

Many people think that "following one's conscience" means doing whatever one thinks is right or wrong, but that is not quite accurate. Individuals who consult their consciences should not be trying to find out their own individual opinions about the morality of an action. Rather, they should be trying to find out what *really is* objectively right or wrong. To speak in Catholic terms, a person should be trying to find out whether an action is in accord with God's will.

So how does a Catholic determine God's will? In question 5 we discuss the importance of the teachings of the Catholic Church on moral issues. Sometimes simply discovering and understanding those teachings is sufficient to determine the moral response to a problem. A Catholic who has the gift of faith is assured that the Holy Spirit guides the Church on matters of faith and morals. For instance, a faithful couple struggling with infertility would rule out in vitro fertilization as a solution to their struggle once they learned the Church's teaching on it (see question 18).

On the other hand, we note that sometimes the Church has no definite or clear teaching on an issue. For instance, an infertile couple may consider "adopting," or having implanted in the wife, an "orphaned" embryo that was created through an in vitro procedure and then abandoned by the natural parents. As of yet there is no definitive Church teaching on this matter (see question 21). A couple would need to decide this matter based on their understanding of Catholic teaching, the guidance of the Holy Spirit and their consciences.

Another example of the need for a decision of the conscience is a situation that requires the application of some known teaching to a particular set of circumstances. For instance, how does one know when a medical procedure is obligatory or optional, such as continued use of a respirator for a dying patient? The Church has guidelines, but each situation requires prayer and honest reflection on the part of those making the decision.

The Church cannot have teachings on every particular situation, since particular situations involve many factors that must be considered. For instance, deciding whether a medical treatment is "ordinary" can involve such factors as the proximity of death, the various family obligations a patient may have and the expense of continued treatment (see question 40). It is not always easy to assess properly all relevant considerations, and in the end conscience must come to a judgment about what is the right thing to do in the concrete situation.

To say that Catholics are free to act in accord with their consciences in matters that are undecided by the Church or in the application of ethical rules to a particular concrete situation is not to say that they can do whatever they want in respect to their decision. Rather, they must form their consciences well and decide in accord with what they in good faith believe God wants them to do. In such cases they first must try to understand the facts of the situation as clearly as possible, for variations in fact greatly influence the morality of situations.

Catholics should consult trusted advisors, perhaps the parish priest or someone who has studied moral theology and bioethics. They might read articles by theologians who have grappled with the issue. The advice of individuals who express a commitment of faithfulness to the Magisterium should carry the most weight.

And as decision makers gather this information, they should pray about their decision. They should make certain that they are in a state of grace: Receiving the sacrament of reconciliation is always helpful! Perhaps they could say a novena to a favorite saint or write a prayer that they could pray for a certain duration, either with others or individually. Once they have prayed, they can be at peace with their decision, since they have tried their best to discover God's will.

Question 5: Are Catholics always obliged to follow Church teaching?

It is important to be clear about what the phrase "Church teaching" means. Most properly it refers to carefully formulated propositions that the Church teaches explicitly and that are to be definitively held by all the faithful. For instance, there is no doubt that the Church teaches that abortion is always wrong, and Catholics are obliged to follow such definitive teaching.

But people also use the phrase to refer to how some thinkers believe principles that have been firmly taught apply to issues for which no magisterial pronouncement exists. For instance, some theologians maintain that the same principles that determine the Church's teaching on abortion would rule out certain treatments of ectopic pregnancies, while others maintain that the same treatments are moral.

Those attempting to learn what the Church teaches about any issue should pay careful attention to the types of sources they consult. We owe a greater level of allegiance to teachings appearing in magisterial documents than to the teachings of individual theologians. Moreover, different types of magisterial documents require different levels of adherence. We will not sort out all the details of these differences here, but we will give some general guidelines to help laypeople assess the status of a teaching.

Bioethical teachings are of several kinds. First there are the foundational principles that bioethics shares with all ethical and moral theology. These are most easily found in the *Catechism of the Catholic Church*, but they also are explained and invoked in various magisterial documents. Principles are fundamental universal truths that are known sometimes by reason alone and sometimes only through revelation. For instance, "Never do moral evil in pursuit of good" is a principle known by reason that governs all ethical thought. The principle "Man should act and treat other human beings as creatures made in the image and likeness of God, destined for eternal union with him through the work of Christ" is known only from revelation.

It is not the responsibility of bioethics to establish or defend these principles; the disciplines of philosophy and theology do that. Bioethics is a discipline that applies these principles to specific health care issues. The Church explains the proper application of these principles in a variety of documents: for instance, the documents issued by councils, such as Vatican Council II; the *Catechism of the Catholic Church*; encyclicals; instructions; exhortations; declarations; papal speeches to various assemblies and documents issued by Curial congregations. Bishops and bishops' conferences also issue statements that bear upon bioethical issues.

Theologians and health care professionals contribute a great deal to the shaping of these teachings. When a new issue arises, such as embryonic stem cell research, theologians and health care professionals often gather in international congresses to discuss how the basic principles of ethics and moral theology apply. Scholars publish books and articles examining and proposing various solutions. Over a period of time—after much consideration, analysis and prayer—positions become clarified. Eventually the proper authorities at the Vatican may determine which position is true and issue a document promulgating or teaching that position.

Before that process is completed, Catholics are free to follow their consciences in taking up one position or another (see question 4). They should consult a faithful priest, physician or theologian—one who is committed to following Church teaching, well educated in the Church's moral principles and up to date on the current debate—for guidance on how to proceed.

Sometimes faithful Catholics disagree on how to apply principles to certain issues. For instance, throughout the nineties there was much disagreement about the moral necessity of providing artificial nutrition and hydration (ANH) to patients in a persistent vegetative state (PVS). In 1990 the Texas bishops issued a statement teaching that it was permissible to withdraw ANH from PVS patients,[5] in 1991 the bishops of Pennsylvania taught that it was not permissible,[6] and in 1992 the Pro-life Committee of the United States Conference of Catholic Bishops (USCCB) advised that, while individuals were free to follow their consciences since there was no authoritative teaching or settled opinion, ANH should be provided as an expression of respect for life.[7]

In 2004, in an address to the International Congress on "Life-Sustaining Treatments and Vegetative State: Scientific Advances and Ethical Dilemmas," Pope John Paul II used very strong and clear language to teach that ANH must "in principle" be provided to PVS patients who are not imminently dying and can assimilate nutrients since it is "care" not "treatment," it is ordinary and not extraordinary and the benefits are proportionate to the burden. Failure to provide it amounts to "euthanasia by omission."[8]

The vehicle for enunciating this teaching and the relative newness of the teaching certainly indicate that the Church has not pronounced it infallibly. Nonetheless, many theologians hold that it is a teaching to which Catholics owe religious submission of intellect and will. Indeed, the Holy Father used language of such precision and force that it seems that his teaching should guide Catholics in respect to providing ANH for those in a PVS. One would expect Catholic health care institutions to adopt the practices the Holy Father advocated.

An example of an undecided issue is the practice of women "adopting" and gestating embryonic human beings who were created as part of an in vitro fertilization procedure and then frozen as "excess" or "spare" embryos. The debate on this matter is currently very lively among committed faithful Catholics who completely agree with each other on fundamental principles. Until the magisterial Church achieves clarity on the issue and promulgates a teaching, Catholics should form their consciences by consulting with trusted advisors and prayerfully considering the advice they receive. See question 21 for more discussion of this issue.

Finally, let us be clear that Catholics do not lose their "freedom" once the Church takes a position on a moral issue; each Catholic must still freely decide to follow that teaching. A decision by the Church provides the clarity and guidance that any responsible person desires. Catholics believe that the Holy Spirit guides the Catholic Church, and thus the Church is a reliable guide to the will of God in matters of faith and morals. It is an inestimable gift to be part of the body of Christ and to work together to advance God's kingdom on this earth. Human dignity and human freedom flourish when we make truth the guide for our actions, rather than our opinions or our perceived needs.

Question 6: If a Catholic in ignorance of Church teaching does something contrary to that teaching, such as using in vitro fertilization, does he or she sin?

The Church teaches that in order to be guilty of sin, a person must know that what he or she is doing is wrong and must do the action willingly. So if a Catholic woman does not know that in vitro fertilization is wrong and uses this method to conceive a child, she is not sinning. She does something that objectively speaking is intrinsically evil, but because of her lack of knowledge, she does not sin: that is, she has no moral culpability.

Another example is that of a very young pregnant girl who has an abortion because her mother insists on it, telling her daughter that what is growing within her is simply undifferentiated tissue. The girl believes the falsehood, knowing no reason not to believe it. She does something that in its kind is intrinsically evil, but she does not sin. The ignorance that excuses wrongdoing is called "invincible ignorance."

There is a kind of ignorance, however, that does not excuse wrongdoing, namely "vincible ignorance." This concept is illustrated well through civil law. If a driver, paying no attention to posted limits, gets stopped for speeding, he cannot plead ignorance as an excuse. Drivers have the responsibility to be informed about laws governing driving, and a failure to become informed about those laws and to pay attention to posted limits is itself wrongful neglect.

Similarly, doctors have an obligation to continue their medical education so that they are aware of the most effective treatments currently available. A failure to be aware of developments in the field of medicine constitutes vincible ignorance for the physician. In other words, vincible ignorance, the ignorance that does not excuse one of wrongdoing, depends upon what a person *can* and *ought* to know.

Mature Catholics of sound mind are obliged to know Church teaching. This does not mean that they are expected to be moral theologians. Yet in modern America, where most people have a high level of education, Catholics have considerable responsibility for educating themselves about Church teaching. Generally, Catholics should learn about Church teaching through their parishes—through homilies, bulletin inserts, lectures and pamphlets in the Church rack.

Catholics can accomplish their duty to further their education by reading Scripture (which will ignite their desire to follow Christ and his Church) and magisterial documents, such as the *Catechism of the Catholic Church* and the abbreviated *Compendium of the Catechism of the Catholic Church*. They also can develop their intellectual formation in the faith by subscribing to Catholic publications and tuning in to Catholic radio and television. They will benefit a great deal from attending local and national conferences on Catholic doctrine.

In general, a person's education in matters of faith should be roughly equal to his or her overall level of education. Unfortunately, it often happens that a person with a sophisticated secular education has the equivalent of a grade-schooler's understanding of the faith. This is true for many doctors, nurses and other professionals. Such a disparity leaves a person both spiritually and intellectually impoverished.

In recent decades there has been much confusion about Church teaching on such matters as contraception and sterilization, since most professional moral theologians have dissented from Church teaching on these issues. Catholics have received the impression that they are free to disobey such teachings, to "follow their own consciences" (see question 4). Sometimes priests have taught couples that they may use contraception or be sterilized. The moral culpability of these misinformed Catholics may be slight or even nonexistent: that is, even though they have been contracepting or have been sterilized, they are not guilty of doing so if they are invincibly ignorant.

People who later discover that they have not been living in accord with Church teaching need to do a careful examination of conscience to determine whether they should have known what the Church teaches on the particular matter. Sometimes confession will not be necessary, but sometimes it will be. Even those who believe themselves to be innocent of wrongdoing would be wise to bring up the matter in the confessional, to clarify any possible confusion or guilt.

While being invincibly ignorant relieves one of moral culpability for wrongdoing, it does not protect one from the likely natural bad consequences of one's action. A young girl who through invincible ignorance has had an abortion will likely suffer some serious life consequences: perhaps some physical or psychological damage from the abortion, confusion about the value of human life or the burden of unearned guilt. Couples who have contracepted out of invincible ignorance will likely not have achieved the level of intimacy that sexual intercourse naturally facilitates or the level of generosity that being open to children facilitates. They also may have deprived themselves of a larger family, which could have been a source of great joy over a lifetime.

Thus Catholics should be motivated to form their consciences for many reasons—among them, concern over the bad consequences that generally follow upon bad actions. But first and foremost they should want to form their consciences out of love for the truth and love for Christ and his Church.

Question 7: What kinds of actions are intrinsically evil?

The Church teaches that some actions are intrinsically evil. Such actions ought never be done, no matter what good consequences might come from them. Intrinsically evil actions are inherently incompatible with the dignity of human persons. Rape, for instance, is intrinsically incompatible with the freedom that should govern human choices, especially about such an intimate part of our being as our sexuality. Even were some great good to be accomplished through a rape (such as satisfying a tyrant who threatens to kill thousands unless the rape is carried out), it should never be done.

We need, however, to be careful about our understanding of the word *evil*. To our modern world the word means something extremely vicious: The Nazi killing of the Jews is a standard example of something truly evil. The Church, however, uses the term *evil* to refer not only to extremely serious moral wrongs but also to anything that does not measure up to what it ought to be.

There are physical evils, ranging from severe deformity to nearsightedness and hangnails. There is also a wide range of intrinsic moral evil, such as stealing millions from a charity versus stealing a candy bar. Similarly, to lie under oath in a murder case is extremely serious; to lie about a trivial matter in casual conversation is much less serious. Both lies are intrinsically evil, but clearly the gravity of the evil is radically different.

Some people think that the Church has a very long list of actions that are intrinsically evil and thus people really have very few decisions to make about moral action: They need only learn what the Church teaches and abide by that. But the Church judges relatively few actions to be evil in themselves: that is, evil because of the kind of actions that they are (for example, murder, adultery, theft and so on).

To speak of an action being a "kind of action" means that it fits into a category that can be evaluated morally. A small lie and a big lie are both "lies," and lies are intrinsically evil as kinds of actions. Some kinds of actions that are intrinsically evil and must never be done are listed in the Ten Commandments, including worshiping false gods, intentionally taking innocent human life (murder), committing adultery and bearing false witness against another.

There is another kind of action that is called "per se"

good: that is, these actions as *kinds* of actions are always good to do. Such actions as feeding the hungry and caring for the poor qualify as per se good. Nonetheless, even some of these actions should not be done in certain circumstances. For example, a father should not give money to feed the hungry if this would leave him unable to feed his own children.

Most actions are neither intrinsically evil nor per se good: rather their moral evaluations are determined by circumstances or the intentions of the persons performing them. For example, in most cases it is wrong to punch someone, but sometimes punching is a good action—for example, in self-defense. So punching is not intrinsically evil, although it is truly evil or wrong when one punches someone who should not be punched.

Similarly, it is normally evil to speak to people in a way that seriously hurts their feelings. In some circumstances, however, hurtful words must be said for a person's own good or for the good of others. For example, "I'm sorry, but I'm not going to marry you after all."

Question 8: What does it mean to say that an action is a matter of "prudential judgment"?

Prudential judgments are those that are made when no intrinsic evil is involved and where there are a variety of possibly good actions that would achieve a good end. These decisions generally require attention to multiple factors relevant to the situation.

For instance, women who are diagnosed with breast cancer often face a range of choices—from a lumpectomy or a mastectomy to various combinations of chemotherapy and radiation. Women with breast cancer morally can choose different treatments, since factors other than medical concerns determine such decisions. That is, a woman whose career depends upon her physiology—say, she is a dancer—might opt for treatment that leaves her breasts intact. On the other hand, a mother with very young children, who does not yet have full-blown cancer but only precancerous cysts, may want more radical surgery as the most certain way to preserve her life.

Prudential judgments require careful consideration of all the concrete, particular circumstances of the person's life.

Question 9: What is the principle of double effect?

The principle of double effect or "double effect reasoning" governs actions that have two or more morally significant effects. This reasoning originates from Thomas Aquinas's reflections on self-defense.[9] Aquinas maintained that a person may kill another in self-defense (good effect), even if the attacker dies as a result of this defense (bad effect). The bad effect, though it may be foreseen, is not the primary intention of the act.

Aquinas's fundamental insights have been formulated into the following four necessary conditions for determining if an action with two significant effects is ethically right:

1. The act itself is not evil.
2. The evil is not a means to the good.
3. The evil is not intended as an end.
4. There is a proportionate reason for allowing the evil effect.

This formulation has become standard among Catholic and non-Catholic authors alike.

How do these conditions apply to actual cases? Let us consider a nonmedical example, the case of bombing during a just war. Sometimes a valuable military target (say, a plant manufacturing chemical weapons) is located near a civilian residential area. Under some circumstances in which highly accurate "smart bombs" are not available, the pilot may be forced to choose between two unappealing options. Either he drops the bombs on the military target (in which case civilian houses nearby will most likely be destroyed), or he forgoes bombing the chemical weapons manufacturing plant (in which case the war is not brought to a swifter end and people may die from the use of chemical weapons made in the plant). What ought he to do?

Consider how the conditions of double effect reasoning apply to the bombing option:

1. The act itself is not evil: Dropping bombs on a military target in a just war is not evil.

2. The evil is not a means to the good: The possible deaths of the civilians are not the means used to secure the destruction of the chemical weapons manufacturing plant.

3. The evil is not intended as an end: The deaths of the civilians are not the remote goal of the bombing. In other words, the pilot is not bombing the plant so that civilians will be killed.

4. There is a proportionate reason for allowing the evil effect: Bringing a war to a swift end and preventing the use of chemical weapons are great goods that

compensate for the loss of innocent human lives as a side effect.

Thus, double effect reasoning shows that the loss of innocent life in the case of bombing, though deeply regrettable, is not the result of an immoral act. Sound ethics forbids the intentional killing of innocent human life but accepts, in extreme circumstances, allowing the innocent to die when that is a side effect of pursuing an extremely important good.

In addition to its use in military matters and individual self-defense, double effect reasoning is widely applicable in medical ethics. Take, for instance, the case of a pregnant woman with cancer of the uterus. Doctors warn her that unless her uterus is removed immediately, she will die. The fetus will not survive the operation.

The woman faces a horrible situation. Either she forgoes a hysterectomy, thereby allowing the cancer to continue to grow and spread, or she has a hysterectomy, in which case the baby she carries will die. It would seem then that she does wrong whatever she chooses: If she chooses to continue the pregnancy, it would seem that she commits suicide in not having the cancer removed; if she chooses to have the hysterectomy, it would seem that she commits the sin of abortion in bringing about the death of her pre-viable baby.

In fact, neither choice is morally wrong. Both are permissible according to the conditions of double effect reasoning. Let's say she chooses to have a hysterectomy:

1. The act itself is not evil: Removing a diseased uterus is morally permissible.

2. The evil is not a means to the good: The death of the baby is not what restores the health of the woman.

3. The evil is not intended as an end: The baby's death is not sought as the goal of the procedure.

4. There is a proportionate reason for allowing the evil effect: It is permissible to allow another person to die if that is necessary to save one's life.

On the other hand, let's say that the woman chooses not to have a hysterectomy. This choice also can be morally licit. Again, consider the conditions of double effect reasoning as applied to this decision:

1. The act itself is not evil: It is not wrong in itself to refuse a medical treatment.

2. The evil is not a means to the good: It is not the woman's death that makes the baby able to live.

3. The evil is not intended as an end: The mother's death is not the goal or motivation behind turning down the treatment.

4. There is a proportionate reason for allowing the evil effect: It is permissible to allow oneself to die if that is necessary to save another person's life.

A woman who finds herself in this unfortunate situation would not be doing something intrinsically evil in either choice. Both choices are morally acceptable in themselves. A mother of several young children may decide that she needs to live to care for those children and thus choose the hysterectomy. Another woman may choose to forgo the hysterectomy because she believes she is called to lay down her life for the life of her child.

Sometimes double effect reasoning can seem like "double think," a way of justifying evil by coming up with a rationalization that allows us to bend the rules. It is true that double effect reasoning can be abused or put to the service of rationalization. This concern is true, however, for virtually any moral rule or system of ethics. The possible abuse of the principle of double effect does not take away from its legitimate use.

It is not always easy to determine how the principle of double effect applies to various problematic situations. But as many answers in this book indicate, the principle is indispensable for helping determine the morality of some options.

Chapter Two

Beginning-of-Life Issues

Question 10: Why is abortion wrong?

Abortion is the most divisive moral and political issue of our time. The differences between the side in favor of it and the side opposing it are very great, but the main difference is not that one side uses reason to discover truth and the other depends upon religion. The Church's teaching on abortion is not simply a matter of revelation, like the Trinity or the full divinity of Christ. Rather, people can come to understand the moral truth about abortion using their powers of reasoning even without the aid of faith, just as they can about rape or theft.

For the sake of simplicity, we will use the term *embryo* for the child in the womb, in this discussion and throughout this book. In actuality the baby in the womb is called an embryo from the time of conception until eight weeks of age; after that he or she is called a fetus. But what is true for the very young baby in the womb certainly holds for the more mature one. We will also generally speak of the "embryonic human being," rather than "the human embryo," since *embryo* properly describes a stage of development, whereas *human being* describes what the embryo truly is.

The issue of abortion comes down to three fundamental questions:

- First, is an embryo a human being?
- Second, is the embryo a person who has *rights*, such as the right to life?
- Third, does a woman's right to free choice trump the right to life of a human being in the womb?

All these questions can be answered without appeal to the Bible, the pope or religion.

The Embryo as a Human Being

While there was a time when some questioned whether an embryo is a human being, science has long established definitively that the embryo is both living and human. The human embryo possesses human DNA, actively self-develops toward human maturity and is scientifically classified as a member of the species *Homo sapiens*. An individual member of the species *Homo sapiens* comes into existence at the completion of the process of fertilization.

After hours of testimony in the United States Senate on the question of when life begins, Senate Bill 158, the "Human Life Bill," summarized the issue this way: "Physicians, biologists, and other scientists agree that *conception marks the beginning of the life of a human being*—a being that is alive and is a member of the human species. There is overwhelming agreement on this point in countless medical, biological, and scientific writings."[1]

The human embryo was not, is not and never could be a member of any other species than the human species. This one organism—from the very beginning of life until death—is always a human being. Some people claim that the embryo is just a *potential* human being, but it is more accurate to say that it is a very small, actual human being with a great deal of potential. Embryonic human beings, fetal human beings, infant human beings, adolescents and adults are all real human beings with potential yet to fulfill.

The Embryo as Person

It is important to establish whether embryonic human beings are *persons*, since *persons* have the right to life. Unlike the first question, this query is not a scientific one but rather a moral or ethical one. Who should be treated with respect? Who has rights?

Here we can distinguish between two kinds of reasons for valuing human beings (see questions 1 and 2). Some thinkers argue that human beings are to be valued because they are *essentially* human and thus by their *very nature* possess some phenomenal powers. A passage in the Declaration of Independence—"All men are endowed by their Creator with certain inalienable rights, and among these are life, liberty and the pursuit of happiness"— reflects this view. (The founders clearly meant by "men" all who qualify as human beings.)

Human beings from the very beginning of their existence have a certain intrinsic nature, which unfolds as they develop. This nature they receive rather than create for themselves. This view of human value, one enshrined in a secular, political document, is identical to that held by the Church, and we shall say more about it momentarily.

In question 1 we discussed a view becoming increasingly dominant in the modern world, the view that only humans who are able to *function* at a certain level have value. Only human beings who can perform certain valuable activities are accorded rights and dignity. Only those with communication skills, self-awareness, self-motivated activity, reasoning ability or the ability to experience pleasure and pain "count" as persons and thus merit respect. This view holds that human beings who are not so equipped do not have the right to live.

If this view were true, many of those who qualify as human under current law would no longer qualify. Equal rights for all people would be an illusion, and in fact the right to life, liberty and happiness of some would be greater (or less) than the right to life, liberty and happiness of others.

Take, for example, the claim that self-awareness is needed in order to be a person. If only those who are self-aware have rights, the human newborn would not have rights, since newborns possess no discernible self-awareness. Indeed, if self-awareness is what makes us valuable, and if some people are much more self-aware than others, then it would seem to follow that the people who are more self-aware would be more valuable.

Furthermore, self-awareness is something that comes and goes based on circumstances. At one moment a person may be self-aware, but then he or she may be in a serious accident or be put under anesthetic for surgery and thus be completely *unaware* of self. If self-awareness is needed for personhood, then do those in surgery (or asleep) cease being persons? Self-awareness can come and go, but personhood is obviously not something that begins each morning when we wake up and ends each night during sleep.

The famous modern ethicist Peter Singer believes that some animals have more rights than some human beings, because some animals, such as healthy, full-grown chimpanzees, function at a higher level than some human beings, such as newborns. His view clearly conflicts with the understanding that human life is sacred.[2]

The Church holds that the value of a human being does not depend upon what he or she is doing or is capable of doing at a given time. It is not because human beings exercise self-awareness, think or make free choices that they are valuable. Rather human beings are valuable because, simply as creatures made in the image and likeness of God, the powers to do these things are written into their nature, whether or not they are able to display those powers.

Some human beings—due to immaturity, deformity, disease, injury from accident or lack of opportunity—may never be able to engage in many of the activities in which adult human beings customarily engage. Yet, just as the reproductive organs remain reproductive organs even though they may not be in the act of reproducing at a given moment, so too human beings are rational animals even though they may not (and in some cases may never) be functioning in a rational way.

The Church teaches that every single human being merits respect. This teaching means that all human persons have the same basic rights, from the moment of conception until the moment of death, whether or not they are able to perform characteristic human activities.

Perhaps the most powerful indicator that all human beings are valuable because of their nature is what history teaches us. Throughout time some human beings have excluded other human beings from belonging fully to the "class" of humans. The Nazis did it to the Jews, men have done it to women, native-born people have done it to foreigners, slave owners did it to slaves. In retrospect we recognize the terrible injustice of stripping human beings of their natural rights and dignity. To be exclusive in determining who is a member of the human family has in every single case been a gross error in ethical judgment.

If there is any question whether we should recognize a human being as a person, history dictates that we err on the side of according rights to those who are powerless and without a voice. In the modern age the prejudice seems to be against tiny human beings, those in the earliest stages of their existence. But size and stage of maturity should no more be criteria of human personhood than race, religion or sex.

Some people note that the punishment of criminals seems to be an exception to the rule that all humans are due respect. In fact, however, it is not. When we punish criminals we still are respecting their rights—including their right to a fair trial and their right to avoid cruel and unusual punishment. Additionally, punishment serves to reaffirm the fact that the criminal has personal responsibility for his or her crime, unlike, say, a tree or a dog that causes harm. The criminal deserves to be punished precisely on account of his or her human dignity as a responsible agent, and thus punishment shows respect for the criminal.

The Right to Choose?

Third, and finally, does a woman's right to choose deserve greater legal protection than the right to life of an unborn child? Some philosophers have been willing to grant that the fetus has a right to life, but they then argue that the right of a woman to control her body outweighs the rights of the unborn child.

A difficulty with this argument is that abortion involves at least two bodies, the body of the woman and the body of the unborn child. The fetal body and the maternal body are two *different* bodies: of different ages, often of different sexes and of different genetic makeup. A fetus is not a part of his or her mother the way a finger is a part of a person; rather the fetus is temporarily living within the mother.

In general, a person's right to control his or her body ends where another person's body begins. "Controlling our bodies" should not involve injuring or harming another person's body. Harming another's body is precisely what takes place in abortion. There are some things we are never free to choose; taking the life of an innocent human being is one of them.

If two rights come into conflict—say, the right to free speech versus the right to safety—the more important right should prevail. Thus no one is permitted to shout "Fire!" in a crowded theater when there is no fire. As noted above, women do not have the right to choose an abortion, but they do have the right to make choices about their lives. Nonetheless, if a woman's right to make free choices about her life comes into conflict with the right to life of the child in her womb, then the right to life should prevail as the more basic and fundamental right. Those who are not alive cannot exercise any freedom—freedom of speech, freedom of bodily movement or any other kind of freedom of the human person. Thus the right to life is the most fundamental and basic right, and the right to make free choices should give way to it. Abortion therefore cannot be morally justified as an exercise of the liberty of a pregnant woman.

Finally, the Church maintains that the relationship between an unborn child and the mother should never be an antagonistic one. Mother Teresa stated,

> The so-called right to abortion has pitted mothers against their children and women against men. It has sown violence and discord at the heart of the most intimate human relationships. It has aggravated the derogation of the father's role in an increasingly fatherless society. It has portrayed the greatest of gifts—a child—as a competitor, an intrusion, and an inconvenience.[3]

A mother naturally is called to love her children; she is the only one who can nurture and care for the child of her womb, a gift that God has entrusted to her.

Question 11: Since an early embryo can split into twins, is an embryo really an individual? Before the brain develops, is an embryo really rational?

Some people claim that since twinning is possible up until implantation—fourteen to sixteen days after fertilization—there is no one individual before that time. This view confuses *individuality* with *indivisibility;* they are not the same thing. Something can be an individual but also be divisible.

For instance, if a flatworm is cut in the proper location, two flatworms emerge. This fact does not mean that the flatworm prior to being cut really was not an individual flatworm. The worm was an individual, an individual with the potential to become two different individual flatworms.

Although human beings cannot twin spontaneously after fourteen to sixteen days beyond conception, twinning remains at least a theoretical possibility even into adulthood. Human cloning, though ethically problematic (see question 19), is simply a form of twinning in which one human being is made from an already existing one. Obviously, the fact that you could (at least theoretically) give rise to a clone or twin of yourself does not mean that you are not now an individual deserving of respect. Similarly, the fact that a human embryo can give rise to a twin does not mean that the human embryo is not now deserving of respect.

Some people also claim that there is no *rational* being until after implantation, because it is only after implantation that the "primitive streak" begins to develop, which is the precursor to the brain. But there is evidence of rationality before the primitive streak appears: Human DNA has written into it the full program of development of the human being, which includes the development of the brain.

Maureen Condic, associate professor of neurobiology and anatomy at the University of Utah School of Medicine, explains why, from the very beginning, the human embryo is a human organism or human being:

> From the earliest stages of development, human embryos clearly function as organisms. Embryos are not merely collections of human cells, but living creatures with all the properties that define any organism as distinct from a group of cells; embryos are capable of growing, maturing, maintaining a physiologic balance between various organ systems, adapting to changing circumstances, and repairing injury. Mere groups of human cells do nothing like this under any circumstances. The embryo generates and organizes distinct tissues that function in a coordinated manner to maintain the continued growth and health of the developing body. Even within the

> fertilized egg itself there are distinct "parts" that must work together—specialized regions of cytoplasm that will give rise to unique derivatives once the fertilized egg divides into separate cells. Embryos are in full possession of the very characteristic that distinguishes a living human being from a dead one: the ability of all cells in the body to function together as an organism, with all parts acting in an integrated manner for the continued life and health of the body as a whole.[4]

It is not biologically true that the human embryo is merely a collection of uncoordinated cells. Unlike a cancerous teratoma, the internal organization of the human embryo and its coordinated development make it an individual organism rather than merely a bunch of cells from which later an organism emerges with the primitive streak.

Those who wish to deny humanity to the human embryo before implantation and before the emergence of the primitive streak call what exists before that time a "pre-embryo." It is important to note that *pre-embryo* is not a scientific term but rather a form of deceptive speech, used to dehumanize human embryos and make lethal experimentation upon them more acceptable. Lee Silver, a professor of molecular biology at Princeton University, describes the deception as follows:

> I'll let you in on a secret. The term pre-embryo has been embraced wholeheartedly by IVF [in vitro fertilization] practitioners for reasons that are political, not scientific. The new term is used to provide an illusion that there is something profoundly different between what we nonmedical biologists still call a six-day-old embryo and what we and everyone else call a sixteen-day-old embryo.
>
> The term pre-embryo is useful in the political arena— where discussions are made about whether to allow early

embryo (now called pre-embryo) experimentation—as well as in the confines of a doctor's office, where it can be used to allay moral concerns that might be expressed by IVF patients. "Don't worry," a doctor might say, "it's only pre-embryos that we're manipulating or freezing. They won't turn into *real* human embryos until after we've put them back into your body."[5]

By speaking of the "pre-embryo," practitioners of in vitro fertilization and advocates of abortion and lethal research on embryos can better disguise the truth of what is taking place: the evils of risking human life and killing human life at its earliest stages of development for the (possible) benefit or convenience of other people.

Question 12: Since an embryo cannot experience pain until several weeks into the pregnancy, would abortion be moral before that time?

Some philosophers, such as Peter Singer, claim that only beings that are able to experience pleasure and pain deserve respect. They reason this way: We do nothing wrong if we kick a rock or a post, but if we kick a dog or a child, it is wrong. What is the difference? The difference is that the dog and the child are *sentient*—they can experience pleasure and pain—while the rock and the post cannot feel anything.

Often this view is supported by utilitarianism, which holds that an act is moral if it brings about the greatest happiness for the greatest number. The utilitarian defines "happiness" as pleasure and lack of pain. So if something cannot experience pleasure or pain, the thought goes, we don't need to worry much about how we treat it. Thus, utilitarians reason that since an unborn child cannot experience pleasure and pain at all stages of development, abortion before sentience develops is not wrong.

There is a grain of truth in this perspective: Namely, we should not inflict *needless* pain on animals or human beings. To inflict pain simply "for the fun of it" is wrong. There are, however, many other ways to harm someone that do not involve physical pain or pleasure or even any psychological pain so it is false to reduce all morality to pleasure and pain. If a person spreads false, malicious rumors about another, he inflicts no physical pain and may not inflict any emotional pain, because the victim may not become aware of what the liar has done. Yet clearly, in lying about another and tarnishing his reputation, the liar has done something wrong whether or not the victim finds out about it. Causing pain to someone is often wrong, but morality goes beyond the requirement not to be a torturer.

In other words, defining morality simply in terms of promoting pleasure and causing pain is inadequate. It is equally faulty to base morality simply on what produces the greatest pleasure for the greatest number. If millions of people greatly enjoyed watching the torture of a small child via the Internet, obviously such an act still would be monstrously wrong. In other words, the accomplishment of the happiness of the greatest number is not sufficient to make an action moral.

We must remember that some of those who qualify as persons do not feel pleasure or pain, and most things that can feel pleasure and pain do not qualify as persons. No one thinks that it is all right to kill a patient under anesthesia for surgery or a patient who has a temporary or permanent disability that prohibits him from experiencing pleasure or pain. On the other hand, making the ability to experience pain the criterion for being a person and having rights would expand the category of personhood in pretty ridiculous ways. We would have to outlaw mousetraps and rat poison!

Indeed, some methods of killing involve no pain, but killing someone in a pain-free way does not make killing permissible. Killing an innocent person is wrong not because it causes pain but rather because it intentionally destroys innocent human life—which human beings possess from the beginning, through all stages of development.

Question 13: Would abortion to relieve the mental distress of a pregnant woman be moral?

No, it would not be morally right to have an abortion in order to relieve mental distress.

There is no doubt that pregnancy may be a time of difficulty and anxiety for some women. However, since the child in the womb is a person, deserving of respect and having fundamental dignity, the mother may not relieve her mental distress by ending her child's life. This would be quite clear in other cases—for instance, where a newborn or other family member might be causing someone distress.

The fundamental moral principle at stake is that evil may not be done that good may come from it. Although a utilitarian would assert that anything is permitted in seeking the greater good, Christian thought is very clear that some acts (such as intentionally killing an innocent human being) may never be chosen licitly.

Considered from another angle, abortion often compounds the mental distress women experience. Many women deeply regret their abortions, feel plagued by guilt and endure mental distress over the abortion well beyond the nine months of a pregnancy.

In situations where a pregnant woman feels intense mental distress, we as Christians need to seek ways to help both the mother and the child. Mental distress can often be lessened through changes in diet, exercise, psychological therapy, massage and, in some serious cases, medication. When some external factor—such as poverty, homelessness or joblessness—is causing a woman mental distress, caring individuals should offer to help her find ways out of these difficulties. The fact that there are more pregnancy help centers in the United States than there are abortion clinics indicates that many generous people are eager to help these women in distress.

Question 14: Is it moral to have an abortion if the unborn child is handicapped?

Although every parent hopes for a healthy child, unfortunately this hope is not always realized. Prenatal diagnosis can reveal that a child developing in the womb has severe mental or physical disabilities. Although prenatal diagnosis can be a wonderful opportunity to begin to initiate treatment for the "second patient," the one within the mother's womb, using it as a tool to select who will live and who will die is an immoral use. Abortion is always morally wrong, even in cases where medical opinion indicates that the child will be born with a disability.

Some people are tempted to turn to abortion as a solution for what they perceive to be "the problem": the disabled infant. The real problem, however, is not the unborn person but his or her diseased condition. In such situations we should seek to alleviate the problematic condition, not get rid of the child with the problem.

Human dignity does not depend upon one's physical condition or health (see question 1). To be sick or gravely handicapped does not undermine the intrinsic dignity of a human being. Philosophically speaking, to choose to kill an innocent human being because of his or her disability is to undermine the foundation of all human dignity, of human equality, which is based not on how we perform or function but rather on who we are: human beings. Many adults with disabilities oppose aborting human fetuses with disabilities: They insist that their own value is diminished and their rights are threatened if the lives of the disabled unborn are threatened.

Theologically speaking, those in need are precisely those to whom we owe the most care and concern. The weak, the sick and the unproductive are those in whom we find the suffering Savior and through whom we have a chance to serve God.

While caring for a disabled child sometimes brings challenges requiring heroic sacrifices, it also can bring incredible gifts. Simon Barnes, the chief sports writer for the *Times* (United Kingdom), says about parenting his son Eddie: "I have a child with Down's syndrome and for that, people pity me. And I am here to say: wrong. Wrong, wrong, wrong. I am not to be pitied but to be envied."[6]

Every child is a gift from God to be treasured. We are here to serve their needs; they do not exist to meet ours, although paradoxically they often do in the most surprising and often delightful ways.

Question 15: Is it immoral to use "excess" embryos for research?

The cells of an embryo are *pluripotent:* this means that they have the potential to develop into many different kinds of cells in the human body. Some researchers believe these pluripotent cells could be helpful in curing or treating many kinds of conditions and diseases, including stroke, spinal cord injury, Parkinson's, Alzheimer's, burns, heart disease, diabetes and rheumatoid arthritis.

Certainly the Church supports scientific research and the development of cures for disease. Indeed, the first hospitals and universities in the world were Church-sponsored, and many of the most prominent scientists of all time were Christians, including Isaac Newton, Johann Kepler and Louis Pasteur. Their desire to learn the truth and cure disease was completely consistent with the Christian faith.

Simply having good goals, however, cannot make an action right. There are some kinds of scientific research that virtually everyone rightly condemns. For example, during World War II Nazi doctors, hoping to obtain information to help others, experimented on Jewish prisoners in numerous ways, including inducing hypothermia and then attempting to revive the victims by various means. Such experiments were grossly wrong, in part because they inflicted pain on individuals who did not consent to the experiments. The argument was made that these individuals were going to die soon and that they could make a contribution to medicine before they died. What was their pain in the face of the benefits that would come to others from the experiments?

We tend to think that only people as horrible as the Nazis could do such things, but researchers in the United States also have failed to recognize the full human rights of other human beings. For instance, the United States Public Health Service, for a forty-year period between 1932 and 1972, conducted a study known as the Tuskegee Experiment. Doctors told nearly four hundred African American men that they were treating them for syphilis. Instead they left the syphilis untreated so that they could study the progress of the disease. These men obviously did not give their consent; many of them led painful lives and died painful deaths. But since they were considered lesser human beings, the researchers believed the experiment justified.

Do the principles violated by the above experiments apply in respect to embryonic stem cell research (ESCR)? Some people think that since the embryonic human being is unable to make free choices, the principle that consent is necessary for experimentation does not apply. They also believe that they would not be harming the embryonic human being, who is unable to feel pain since its nervous system is undeveloped (see question 12).

ESCR violates an even more fundamental principle than those of consent and pain. It violates the principle that we should not kill the innocent.

As currently practiced, the harvesting of stem cells from an embryonic human being involves the destruction of a very tiny human being. As we explained in question 11, a human embryo is nothing other than a human person in the first stage of human development. As a person, the embryo deserves to be treated with respect. Killing one innocent human being in order to (potentially) benefit other human beings is wrong. Thus, ESCR as currently practiced is wrong.

Often ESCR takes place on so-called "spare embryos," those that are left over from attempts at in vitro fertilization and that the mother does not intend to gestate. Since the embryos will die anyway, one argument in favor of ESCR is that this research at least brings something good out of what would otherwise be a total loss.

The fact that some embryos likely will die anyway does not, however, justify ESCR. We can imagine adults with fatal diseases or inmates on death row who are equally "doomed to die," but we cannot use them for our purposes as if they lacked humanity. Were we to do so we would be acting as the Nazis and the Tuskegee researchers did.

Similarly, it is wrong to disrespect an embryonic human by killing him or her (remember that from conception the sex of the embryo is determined as male or female) to help others. He or she already has suffered terrible disrespect in having been made in a petri dish rather than through an act of love between the mother and father.

It must also be noted that some scientists believe ESCR is not a very promising avenue for actual cures because it is currently not possible and may never be possible to direct the growth of embryonic stem cells precisely. Such cells tend to grow into a disorganized mass of tissue, a teratoma, rather than follow an organized and healthy pattern of development.[7]

Too few people seem to know that adult stem cells have already been a source of cures.[8] An adult stem cell is not a cell necessarily taken from an adult; adult stem cells are found in the bodies of infants as well as adults; they are more mature than embryonic stem cells and also more limited. While further research may demonstrate that they are able to become as elastic as embryonic stem cells, currently they are considered to be *multipotent*. This means they can develop into several different kinds of body cells.

Adult stem cells have proven to be effective in treating dozens of conditions for several reasons. It is of great benefit that individuals can use genetically compatible cells from their own bodies, since these cells do not prompt an immune system response. If genetically incompatible cells are used, there is a subsequent need for immunosuppressive drugs, which themselves bring harmful side effects to the patient. In addition, these adult stem cells also do not exhibit the rapid and uncontrollable growth of embryonic stem cells that results in tumors.

There is another method of getting embryonic stem cells, which some scientists maintain does not involve killing an embryo. It goes by the acronym ANT-OAR (Altered Nuclear Transfer-Oocyte Assisted Reprogramming). This process involves what is called "epigenetic programming." The scientist takes a human cell, such as a skin cell, and alters the DNA of its nucleus to limit its future development. This cell, with its altered DNA, is then fused with an egg whose nucleus has been removed. The result is a new cell, a hybrid of the earlier cells, that develops much like an embryo and can be the source of embryonic stem cells. Advocates of ANT-OAR argue that the being created through this process is not an embryonic human being because it can develop only into a teratoma-like entity—that is, a kind of tumor made up of human genetic material that never was a real human embryo.[9]

Yet some respected ethicists oppose ANT-OAR because they believe the process creates a new embryonic human being that from the start is deformed,[10] one that quickly dies yet continues to develop as a tumor.

Other ethicists argue that since it is not certain what exactly is produced through ANT-OAR, the being in question should not be killed until the question of its humanity is clarified.[11]

Although it is possible that researchers may find a moral way to retrieve embryonic stem cells, they must respect the humanity of the embryo. Currently there are no procedures that uncontroversially pass that nonnegotiable test, but it is hoped that new procedures may be found. For example, stem cells taken from amniotic fluid, without killing any embryos, may provide a morally permissible way to do embryonic stem cell research.

Question 16: Which ways of treating ectopic pregnancies are moral?

Ectopic pregnancies (more and more frequent because of scarring caused by sexually transmitted diseases) are life threatening. In most cases of ectopic pregnancy, an embryonic human being begins to grow in a fallopian tube rather than in the womb, and as it grows it threatens to cause the tube to rupture, which could cause the mother to bleed to death.

Before discussing the morality of methods for treating ectopic pregnancies, let us note that in the vast majority of cases the embryo dies without any intervention. Moreover, it is impossible for an embryo to develop to viability within the fallopian tube. Current treatments typically result in the death of the embryo. Reports of successful transfers of embryos from the fallopian tube to the uterus are extremely rare.[12]

Ways of treating ectopic pregnancies are examples of the application of the principle of double effect: the principle that permits us to do things that have both good and bad effects as long as one does not do evil directly to achieve good, and the good sought is proportionate to the foreseen but tolerated evil (see question 9). Until techniques for transferring embryos to the uterus are perfected, all efforts need to be directed to trying to save the mother—obviously a good "effect" or goal to have. Yet just because a baby is going to die anyway does not mean that we can kill him or her; we may never *directly* kill an innocent human being.

To speak of Church teaching on dealing with ectopic pregnancies is, for the most part, to speak of what has become a practice approved by Catholic doctors and theologians faithful to Catholic moral teaching. The Magisterium has not yet made a determination about which contemporary treatments for ectopic pregnancies are morally right or wrong.

For decades faithful Catholic doctors have been performing *salpingectomies*, procedures that cut out the "diseased" portion of the tube: that is, the portion that is at risk of rupturing. Encased in that portion of the tube is an embryonic human being, who dies when that portion of the tube is removed from the mother. The baby is not attacked directly, and thus the death of the baby is a "double effect" of the procedure. The doctor does not kill the baby so that the mother might live; rather he does a procedure to save the mother that also as a side effect results in the death of the child.

A problem with a salpingectomy is that the woman loses some of her fertility because she loses use of the severed tube. Precisely for that reason doctors have tried to find procedures that will both save the woman's life and preserve her fertility. A *salpingostomy* is one of these procedures. In this procedure the doctor makes an incision in the tube and removes the embryonic human being, who dies as a result of the removal. The tube is then repaired, and the mother's fertility is preserved.

Another treatment that preserves fertility is the use of the drug *methotrexate*. It is a powerful drug, sometimes used in cancer treatments. Basically methotrexate dissolves the tissue by which the embryo is attached to the fallopian tube, and the embryo then washes out of the tube. This procedure can be done without damaging the fallopian tube, though some of the side effects are potentially serious for the woman. The unborn child always dies.

The obvious question arises: Do a salpingostomy and the use of methotrexate involve a direct attack on the embryo: that is, would a doctor who does them be performing an abortion to save the life of the mother? Most faithful doctors and theologians reject these methods because they believe that they directly kill embryonic human beings.

A minority of faithful theologians argues that salpingostomy, the procedure that removes the embryo but keeps the tube intact, does not involve a direct attack on the embryonic human being. Rather, they maintain that the procedure is properly described as an act directed to saving the mother's life by performing a "rescue mission" for the embryo. Since theoretically the embryo might live, the act is not directed at killing the embryonic human being.

With the current state of technology, this "rescue mission" always fails: The baby never lives. But the baby cannot live in the fallopian tube either; leaving the embryo there does not save his or her life. The embryo does not belong in the fallopian tube; and while it remains there, the life of the mother is at risk.

Perhaps someday medical technology will provide the possibility of transferring the embryo to the mother's womb or an artificial womb.[13] This is the hope of the medical community and the Church. Presently we cannot complete the "rescue mission," but some think we should do the portion of it that we can. In doing so we remove the embryo from a place where he or she cannot live anyway and thereby save the life of the mother.

A very small minority of faithful theologians argues that methotrexate does not cause a direct abortion. They claim that methotrexate attacks the cells (the forerunner to the placenta—the trophoblast) that attach the embryo to the tube and not the embryo itself. The trophoblast, they claim, is not really an organ of the embryo. Methotrexate is not a "direct" or "intentional" attack on the embryo but rather an attack on a pathology, with the unfortunate side effect of the death of the embryonic human being.

Opponents of methotrexate counter that attacking the portion of the body that supplies nutrition is a direct attack on life. Further, they claim that it is likely that the whole embryo is being attacked: that is, that the methotrexate kills embryonic cells also.

Since the morality of various forms of treatment of ectopic pregnancy remains a matter of debate among ethicists in the Catholic tradition faithful to the Magisterium, physicians and patients faced with these pregnancies must form their consciences carefully and pray ardently for guidance (see question 4).[14]

Question 17: Is it ever morally permissible to induce labor prematurely?

Inducing labor prior to the due date when there is no significant health risk for the unborn child is not morally problematic. One could imagine this being done for a variety of reasons: for example, allowing a father who is leaving for military service to be present for the birth.

In some cases premature induction is to the benefit of the unborn child; in fact, sometimes it can be the only way to save the life of an unborn child. Consider the case of a pregnant woman badly injured in a car accident who appears to be dying. Her death may threaten the baby's access to oxygen. Removal may be in the best interest of the unborn child and may also, at least theoretically, be advantageous to the mother, whose bodily systems might be strained by pregnancy.

Ethical questions arise in the situation in which prematurely induced labor would put an unborn child's health at risk. For example, what if a woman is told—because of some physical condition, perhaps some problem with her kidney—that she will not (or may not) survive pregnancy unless labor is induced?

In cases that seemingly pit the well-being of the mother against the well-being of her baby, the principle of double effect is relevant. As discussed in question 9, double effect reasoning requires that:

1. The act itself is not evil.
2. The evil is not a means to the good.
3. The evil is not intended as an end.
4. There is a proportionate reason for allowing the evil effect.

The act of inducing labor is not wrong in itself: It is not an intrinsic evil like adultery, murder or idolatry. Of course, if the induction of labor is simply a means of terminating pregnancy (intentionally killing the unborn prior to viability), it is intrinsically wrong. The ill effects that are endured by the fetus are not a means to the good effects for the mother: It is not as if the organs of the baby are being harvested for the mother's good. The evil effects for the baby are not intended as an end. It remains to ask: Is there a proportionate reason for allowing the evil effect?

Here the matter would have to be assessed clinically. Obviously, if the beneficial effects for the woman were negligible and the likely or certain harm to the unborn child serious, then the answer must be that there is no proportionate reason. If the benefit to the woman were great, however, such as saving her life, then there would be a proportionate reason for allowing, regrettably, the risk of some harm to the child.

What about cases where the unborn child is thriving in the womb but will die shortly after birth? In cases of anencephaly, for example—in which the brain of the unborn child is not properly developed or virtually absent—the death of the child shortly after birth is a practical certainty. If the continued presence of a deformed child in the womb presents some serious physical health risks to the mother, premature delivery may be morally permissible according to the criteria laid out above. Yet often the continued presence of the deformed child presents no threat to the physical health of the mother. Some doctors believe that carrying to term a severely deformed child, one destined to die soon after birth, could cause undue psychological stress on the mother, and they recommend premature induction of labor.

In 1996 the USCCB explicitly addressed this situation in their document "Moral Principles Concerning Infants With Anencephaly." They wrote:

> It is clear that before "viability" it is never permitted to terminate the gestation of an anencephalic child as the *means* of avoiding psychological or physical risks to the mother. Nor is such termination permitted after "viability" if early delivery endangers the child's life due to complications of prematurity. In such cases, it cannot reasonably be maintained that such a termination is simply a side-effect of the treatment of a pathology of the mother.[15]

When a baby has anencephaly, it is the baby, not the mother, who is suffering from the malformation. The mother is not diseased and cannot possibly maintain that she needs an abortion for her physical health. It is wrong to kill the anencephalic infant in the womb or to risk shortening the already short life of the anencephalic infant by exposing him or her to the dangers that come with premature delivery.

Mothers who know their babies are anencephalic understandably suffer enormous stress. They can, however, learn to communicate their love to the child in the womb and to treasure this short period of time granted them to love this needy infant.

CHAPTER THREE

Reproductive Technologies

Question 18: Which reproductive technologies are moral?

The Church teaches that two fundamental values must be respected when seeking to conceive a child: the dignity of the child conceived and the meaning of marriage.[1] Methods that endanger the life or well-being or dignity of the child conceived are immoral. So too are methods by which spouses become parents other than by each other—either using someone else's sperm, egg or womb or having a technician be the immediate cause of impregnation. The conception of new life takes place morally only as a direct act of marital intercourse.

It is perfectly right for childless spouses to seek a remedy to their childlessness, since the desire to have a child is natural and children are fulfilling of marriage. Indeed, infertility is a very great cross. Nonetheless it is not true that spouses have a *right* to a child. A child is always a *gift* and must be respected as a gift. Couples have to choose morally acceptable means to receive what it is natural for them to want.

The Church does not disapprove of any measures simply because they are artificial. Indeed, it approves of artificial measures that *assist* the spouses in achieving a pregnancy as a *direct* result of an act of marital intercourse.

It is moral to use artificial means to *restore* fertility. Sometimes a husband or wife has physical maladies that can be corrected. For instance, various surgeries or treatments can help men produce more sperm or clear up anomalies; women may have surgery or take drugs to clear up endometriosis or ovarian cysts. Women may take fertility drugs that enable them to ovulate, as well as hormones that enable them to sustain a pregnancy.

In restoring individuals to healthier conditions, such measures can enable spouses to achieve pregnancy through an act of spousal intercourse.[2] Here we have what is "artificial" (surgery, drugs) *assisting* rather than *replacing* nature. And of course, simply learning fertility awareness—that is, Natural Family Planning, by which a woman determines when she is ovulating—is immensely helpful in achieving pregnancy.

Methods of reproduction that violate or replace nature are becoming increasingly popular. Artificial insemination, a fairly common procedure, involves acquiring semen (generally through masturbation) and injecting it into a woman's reproductive system at a time coinciding with ovulation. The semen can come from the woman's husband (or "partner") or from a donor or seller.

The most common reproductive technology is in vitro fertilization (IVF).[3] The procedure sometimes uses the egg of the woman to be impregnated and sperm from her husband. It also can involve donated or purchased eggs, donated or purchased sperm, sometimes even the services of a surrogate mother and various combinations of these.

To get enough eggs for the procedure, a woman undergoes a process called *hyperovulation*. She must take fertility drugs to produce a large number of eggs, often causing serious physical side effects. A doctor then removes the eggs from the ovaries through ultrasound aspiration or laparoscopy.

Although there are moral ways to obtain semen (it is moral to use a perforated condom during a marital act of sexual intercourse), the male generally masturbates to do this—a violation of sexual ethics. Sperm are then separated from the semen and formed into a pellet through centrifugal spinning. Sperm and eggs are then combined in a petri dish to produce several embryonic human beings, some of which are implanted.

The remainder, those not chosen for implantation—the "excess embryos"—are either discarded, frozen, donated to others or used for research. Women who become pregnant with more than one fetus sometimes "selectively terminate"—that is, abort—the unborn child or children who are not wanted.

Another method, called GIFT (gamete intrafallopian transfer), involves removing eggs from the ovaries and placing them in the fallopian tube along with sperm. The conception takes place in the fallopian tube. For a description of other methods, check the Web site of the Centers for Disease Control.[4]

There is no centralized, reliable source for records on these various procedures, but most commentators believe the success rate is not over 30 percent, a low rate that generally leads to multiple, expensive attempts. The whole process can put considerable strain on a relationship because of the expense and the heartbreak of failed attempts. In comparison to natural reproduction, IVF carries a much higher risk of birth defects, such as anomalies of the sex organs, clubfeet, extra fingers and toes and mental retardation.[5]

Perhaps the descriptions above serve to indicate why the Church rejects these technologies. In these procedures a child is conceived apart from a direct act of spousal intercourse, and thus the child can be considered a product of technical expertise rather than a gift flowing from the complete self-giving that spousal intercourse is meant to be. Although a child who is conceived through artificial technologies has dignity equal to every other human being, that child has been treated like a product in his or her conception and thus not shown proper respect.

The number and variety of lawsuits that have arisen from uncertain parentage associated with these procedures illuminate some of the moral problems involved. For instance, women have sued non-spouse donors or sellers for child support; embryos have figured as property in divorce suits; embryos have been implanted in the wrong woman.

We need to consider the fact that there are some things that one should never delegate to another. For instance, a husband should not have his best friend take his wife out to celebrate their wedding anniversary or send his secretary to see his child's school play in place of himself. Obviously, spouses should reserve sexual activity for each other alone, and it would never be acceptable to "substitute" someone else in the act of sexual intercourse. Likewise, spouses should become parents only through each other.

Some might object that adoption also violates the principle that spouses should become parents only by each other. But adoption does not involve creating a child from the genetic material of others. Loving couples adopt children whose parents because of unfortunate circumstances are not able to raise them.

The practice of donating or selling sperm or egg is also morally wrong. To deliberately allow babies to be "made" from one's genetic material and to not be involved in the lives of those children is to create a problematic situation, one in which a child is not raised by his or her own natural parents. Thus people should not donate or sell their sperm or eggs. Surrogate mothers misuse their reproductive powers, which should serve to gestate the babies conceived by their own husbands. (See question 21 for a possible legitimate exception to this principle.) Moreover, surrogates are generally financially exploited for their services.

Again, the struggle with infertility is one of the many heavy crosses that people bear in this world. We should pray for those who face this struggle and help them find moral ways to meet their needs.

Many couples generously decide to adopt children, an option that is currently more than a little challenging, since abortion has reduced greatly the availability of newborns. It would be wonderful if more couples would consider adopting older children, since such children sometimes spend a lifetime being shifted from foster home to foster home. Those who adopt children from foreign countries often rescue them from a dismal future.

Question 19: Is cloning wrong?

Cloning involves production of a living being by a procedure known as *somatic cell nuclear transfer*. Genetic material from the nucleus of a donor parent cell is placed into an egg from which the nucleus has been removed. When the new entity is properly stimulated, cell divisions begin, and the result is a new being that is an identical twin of the donor, but of course younger in chronological age.

Ethicists debate about whether cloning is acceptable for any living thing, but here we will focus on the cloning of human beings. Human cloning is divided into two kinds: *therapeutic cloning*, in which a new human being is made in order to supply "parts" for the benefit of another; and *reproductive cloning*, in which a new human being is made with the desire to bring the baby to term. Human cloning of both kinds is morally wrong for a number of reasons.

Both kinds of cloning involve creating a human being outside the loving act of a man and woman in marriage (for more on this see question 18). As such, both kinds of cloning contradict the Church's vision of human procreation. In addition, cloning as now practiced subjects the human beings created to serious risks without their consent and not for their benefit.

Therapeutic cloning makes lethal use of one human being as a means of achieving some goal for another human being. Some people want to clone themselves so that they will have a ready source of organs or tissues that are genetically identical to their own. To create and then to kill a human reduces that person to mere "material" for the use of others. Like abortion and lethal embryonic research, therapeutic cloning involves intentionally killing an innocent human being. This is always wrong.

Reproductive cloning is also wrong. The reasons for reproductive cloning are ethically suspect. Those who desire to clone themselves sometimes want to see how someone just like them genetically might develop differently from how they did. They may want the clones of themselves to develop talents they never did. Surely such curiosity is very selfish.

Further, reproductive cloning subjects a child to unknown risks. Among cloned animals there is a much higher rate of death, deformity and disability than among animals brought about by normal intercourse. To subject a human child to such risks is seriously wrong. Moreover, a cloned child will not have two biological parents, a proven natural good of which he or she should not be deprived.

Writers have imagined the risks involved if human beings are designed and grown to maturity simply for the use of others. Huxley's *Brave New World* and Lucas's *Star Wars Episode II: Attack of the Clones* depict scenarios in which human beings are reproduced and altered genetically to make soldiers.

Cloning of either kind—therapeutic or reproductive— should not be practiced, for both constitute offenses to human dignity.

Question 20: Is it moral to have a baby to provide for the medical needs of an already existing child?

Some parents who have a child with a life-threatening condition consider having another baby to provide for certain medical needs of the child who is ill. For instance, a second baby could supply bone marrow for treatment for a first baby with cancer. Or the blood in the umbilical cord of the second baby might provide stem cells that would help the sick child. Are the parents guilty of disrespecting the dignity and intrinsic value of the second baby, of using the second baby as a means to help the first?

The answer to this question in some cases could be yes. Certainly, if the parents have no love for the second baby and have no concern for his or her well-being, they would be guilty of treating that baby as an instrument rather than a person.

Having a second baby to help a first, however, would not be intrinsically evil. Parents have babies for all sorts of reasons: They want a brother or a sister for an existing child; they need more workers on the farm; they want not only girls but boys as well, or vice versa. Ideally at least, the family is a school of generosity that teaches children how to care for each other.

There are limits to such help, of course. Certainly nothing should be done to a second child to put him or her at great risk for the first.

The morality of permitting a minor child, perhaps even a very young child, to donate an organ for a sibling is also an issue. Some hold that to have a child donate replaceable resources, such as blood or bone marrow, would be moral, but to have a child below the age of consent donate an irreplaceable resource, such as a kidney, would be immoral.

A key factor in considering such cases is the amount of risk involved. If helping another seriously risks the well-being of the donor, then the donor must consent voluntarily before the procedure can be done. One cannot volunteer another person for heroic generosity; one can volunteer only oneself. On the other hand, if serious risks are not involved, then parents may "volunteer" a sibling to help another, as happens virtually daily in families. The parents, in consultation with medical personnel, should determine what constitutes a serious risk.

Question 21: Is it morally permissible to "adopt" a frozen embryo?

The widespread practice of in vitro fertilization (IVF) has left hundreds of thousands of embryos frozen in clinics. Some of these may be used for future attempts at implantation or for research; others may be discarded. Still others may be implanted in another woman's womb, where they gestate to maturity.

There has been no official statement at any level in the Church about this practice, generally known as embryo adoption (EA). Theologians are currently debating the topic.

Some of those who oppose EA argue that a wife should get pregnant only by her husband. Others do not consider the practice of implanting embryos into the uterus of women who are not their biological mothers to be "adoption": rather, they think it to be a form of surrogacy, a practice condemned in *Donum Vitae*.[6] Still others think the practice may not be wrong in principle but is wrong as a matter of complicity with evil. That is, having a way of rescuing "excess" embryos provides practitioners of IVF one more reason not to stop what they are doing.

Others support rescuing embryos through embryo adoption. They think the practice serves to recognize the humanity of the frozen embryo. They believe that a wife should not conceive a child by someone other than her husband but that gestating an embryonic human being is similar to breast-feeding another woman's baby: The woman gestating the baby is providing him or her with shelter and food. They claim that this is not the same as the surrogacy of which *Donum Vitae* disapproves: It is not commercial surrogacy or the surrogacy involved directly with artificial insemination or IVF. While the problem of cooperating with the IVF industry is troublesome, an analogy to adopting embryos could be buying slaves from slave owners.

Couples considering this option should read articles by theologians on both sides and then embark on the prayer and discernment program advised in question 5.[7]

Question 22: Is it moral to attempt to have a child when genetic factors make it likely that the child may be mentally or physically handicapped?

Modern medicine allows for choices that were unknown in the past. Couples can now get genetic counseling to determine whether or not it is likely that their children will have malformations or diseases that are genetic in origin. This allows them the choice to have or not have children.

Some people argue that couples should accept whatever children God sends them. Others argue that it would be wrong knowingly to risk having children who might face lives of enormous difficulty and suffering. The Church has no formal teaching on this matter, but it does teach that all human life, no matter how compromised, is of inestimable value. The child with special needs has an immortal soul and an eternal destiny.

It seems that parents who believe that they are capable of meeting the demands of a child with special needs may risk having such a child. Our culture is in desperate need of generous and self-sacrificing witnesses to the goodness of life. Families with special needs children frequently report that those children are a great gift to the whole family. They teach other members of the family how to be selfless and loving.

Yet it would not be immoral for parents to try to avoid pregnancy if they believe that they would find the effort to care for such children overwhelming. Indeed, Pope Pius XII maintained that couples could choose to use periodic abstinence throughout the whole of their marriage to avoid passing on genetic anomalies.[8] Such a decision would not invalidate a marriage, because it does not amount to a refusal to have children: These couples would lovingly accept a child should a pregnancy occur in spite of their practice of Natural Family Planning.

Question 23: Is it moral to try to select the sex of one's baby?

Parents may want to select the sex of their babies for several reasons. They may want to prevent the transmission of a genetic disease that is more common in one sex than another. They may want a male child to carry on the family name or to meet the requirements of their religion. Or they may simply want to achieve some balance within the family.

If sex selection could be done naturally—that is, without involving any of the reproductive technologies that require killing embryonic human beings and without harming children—the Church would not consider it to be intrinsically evil. That is, there can be good reasons for seeking a child of one sex or another, as long as the parents accept whatever child they conceive as an inestimable gift from God.

Nearly all of the known methods of sex selection involve immoral practices: infanticide (a common practice in some countries, such as China); selective abortion or killing of the baby of the "wrong sex" within the womb; creating many embryos and implanting only those of the desired sex; and "sperm sorting," which also involves artificial insemination or IVF.

A natural way to increase the possibility of having a child of one sex or the other could be through timing of intercourse. Practitioners of Natural Family Planning have various theories on how to do this, though these have not yet been verified.

Still, even with natural methods, sex selection may be harmful to the common good. What might be moral for an individual can have serious repercussions for sexual demographics. Nature produces about 105 males for every 100 females. This natural imbalance evens out when a generation reaches marriageable age, because boys tend to die from reckless behavior and disease more often than girls. The practice of sex selection has already disturbed that balance.

Nearly 90 percent of the sex selection that is done worldwide aims at producing male children. Some countries have a gross imbalance between males and females: China, for instance, has roughly 120 males for every 100 females.[9] These cultures may be facing increased crime rates, greater incidence of prostitution and problems with various addictions among males who will never have the opportunity to assume the domesticating responsibilities of marriage.

Question 24: Are ovarian transplants morally permissible?

Some women are born without ovaries, or they have their ovaries removed or destroyed because of a medical condition such as cancer. While the Church would like to help every individual who suffers with infertility, it endorses only moral means for this.

Certainly the ability to transplant organs is in general a good thing. In transplant procedures the organs that once belonged to the donor become the organs of a needy recipient. Some might consider transplantation of an ovary to be morally permissible, since any future pregnancy would be the result of a completed act of conjugal intercourse, which is a requirement of *Donum Vitae* (see question 18). What is morally problematic is that the eggs in the ovaries are not those of the woman receiving them, and *Donum Vitae* teaches against using eggs of those to whom one is not married.[10]

In procreating with her husband, a wife is to share with him what is truly hers, what is imprinted with her personal characteristics. Any child conceived with donated eggs would have the genetic makeup of the donor and would not be the genetic child of the wife. Although the Church's Magisterium has not addressed this issue, it would seem to follow from principles that have been articulated that ovarian transplants (for reproductive purposes) would be immoral.

Some argue that it would be moral to transplant ovaries for the purpose of providing a woman with the hormones she needs to avoid menopausal symptoms. Transplantation of ovaries is not the only source of such hormones; for years women have been taking hormone replacement therapy, although the increased risk of cancer that accompanies such hormonal use makes such use not an altogether attractive option. But the potentially bad side effects of ovarian transplants may be worse, since immunosuppressant drugs may be necessary. Moreover, if the woman receiving the transplant is sexually active, she would, of course, risk becoming pregnant by means of another woman's ovum, and it would seem that risk is not proportionate to the relief of menopausal symptoms. The Church has no teaching on this matter.

The procedure of transplanting ovaries may, however, have a moral application that would be acceptable. It may be possible for a woman whose ovaries would be destroyed by some medical treatment such as chemotherapy to have them removed, frozen and then returned to her own body. The morality of such a procedure would depend upon the risk to her ovaries because of treatment and the likelihood of success with the return of the ovaries to her body, but in itself it would not be intrinsically evil. It would be a marvelous solution to a problem.

CHAPTER FOUR

Contraception, Sterilization and Natural Family Planning

Question 25: Why does the Church teach that contraception is intrinsically immoral?

Contraception is wrong because it damages our physical well-being, our psychological well-being, our marital relationships and our relationship with God.[1]

Until 1930 all Christian churches and some famous religious leaders, including Gandhi, opposed contraception.[2] Much of the argument against contraception was that it would lead to sexual promiscuity and would damage marriages. It is easy to see that those assessments have proved accurate.

The widespread use of contraception in our time is arguably a major cause of societal dysfunction. Since the contraceptive pill was invented in the late 1950s, we have reached the point where about one-fourth of the babies conceived in the United States are aborted and over a third are born to single women. Today one in five Americans has an incurable sexual disease. The majority of couples cohabit before marriage, and these divorce at a much higher rate than those who do not cohabit. Children raised by single parents often live in poverty, suffer from depression and addiction, commit crimes and have unwed pregnancies, abortions and divorces at rates higher than those of children raised by both parents.[3]

Some people may not see any causal connection between these distressing phenomena and contraception; at best they see a correlation. Contraception, however, has changed radically our understanding of the meaning, purpose and proper morality of sexuality. Contraception enables people to sever conceptually—though not completely physiologically—the connection between having sex and having babies.

In the not-so-distant past people generally thought that couples should not have sexual intercourse unless they were in love and prepared for babies, and thus they should reserve sexual intercourse for marriage. Even if couples did not live up to this ideal, the expectation of society was that sexual intercourse was appropriate only in marriage.

Today many people think that there need be no connection between having sex and being in love, let alone being married. Almost everyone who gets married has been sexually active and often with multiple partners, partners whom they may not have loved, with whom they did not want to have children and whom they did not want to marry. Over 50 percent of women going to abortion clinics were using contraceptives when they became pregnant; nearly the whole of the other 50 percent are "contraceptively experienced."

Contraception leads people to think that they can have sex with no preparation or expectation of the responsibility of parenthood. It launches them on a lifestyle that treats sexual intercourse as simply a pleasurable activity to be enjoyed by individuals "ready" for sex—but not necessarily for children or marriage. In spite of the use of contraceptives, unanticipated pregnancies often happen. Thus there is a connection between contraception and unwed pregnancy, abortion, single parenthood and poverty.

The connection between contraception and divorce is likely manifold. Contracepting couples tend to have fewer children, and divorce has been collated with paucity of children.[4] Contraception may also interfere with what was once called "courtship" by accelerating the sexual relationship which is viewed as unlikely to have permanent consequences before they have developed a deep personal relationship founded upon mutual knowledge of each other and shared values.

The cohabitation that precedes many marriages is not a good preparation for marriage.[5] Cohabiting couples often fail to address questions that would challenge the relationship. They do not want to risk breaking up, since that would necessitate splitting up their possessions and starting all over again. They instead "coast" into marriage.

Many modern couples have contracepted sex with multiple partners before marriage. They contracept when they get married, they stop for a short period of time to conceive a child and then they contracept again. They might stop contracepting to have another child and then become sterilized. (Sterilization is the most common form of contraception in the United States.) These couples never have a sustained period of sexual relations of the sort the Church approves: sex between a man and a woman who understand sex to be an expression of complete self-giving, exclusive to one's spouse and open to children.

Many couples get pregnant in spite of using contraceptives and then speak of the pregnancy as an "accident," whereas truly it is not possible to get pregnant by accident.

To get pregnant as a result of sexual intercourse means something has gone right, not that something has gone wrong.

These would be sufficient reasons to be wary of any claims that contraception improves our lives or solves societal problems. We have been a contraceptive culture for decades now, with contraceptive options and availability continually on the rise, and societal dysfunctions appear to mirror that rise.

We should not be surprised at the bad effects of chemical contraceptives, since fertility is a healthy condition that contraceptives treat as though it were a disease. Women do not like the weight gain and the increased propensity to irritability and depression that come with the chemical contraceptives, not to mention the less common but more troublesome migraine headaches, ovarian cysts and other maladies. Some studies link the use of contraceptives with a higher incidence of several kinds of cancer[6] and cardiovascular disease, though there is division on this issue in the scientific community.

Since contraception is generally taken to facilitate sexual intercourse, it is ironic that chemical contraceptives seriously diminish a woman's libido, and thus she does not receive the pleasure she should from the sexual act. Some studies have indicated that the pill distorts a woman's judgment of men: that is, a woman on a hormonal contraceptive generally chooses a different sort of man for a partner than she does when not on a hormonal contraceptive, and this man is generally a less suitable partner for her. Often when women go off the pill, their libido increases but not for their current partner. [7]

Men are more attracted to women in their fertile phase,[8] and women using hormonal contraceptives have no fertile phase. To take children out of the sexual equation (or at least to intend to) changes how both parties in the relationship perceive sexual acts—making negligible the considerations that formerly were involved, such as, would this man (or woman) make a good father (or mother)? Thus, in many ways, hormonal contraceptives have a significant impact on relationships.

The above reasons may be sufficient to raise questions in the minds of many about contraception. While bad physical and psychological effects are in part why the Church condemns it, primarily the Church finds that contraception violates the goods of marriage. The *Catechism of the Catholic Church* states that marriage "is by its nature ordered toward the good of the spouses and the procreation...of offspring" (*CCC*, 1601).

The Church views the healthy and natural functioning of the human body, including its reproductive function, as a great good. Indeed, precisely because the human person is of such inestimable value, the sources of the human person—the fertility of both men and women—also have great value. The Church teaches that sexual intercourse is a kind of "body language": It is properly an expression of love and lifetime commitment. It is meant to be an act of complete self-giving, which includes giving one's fertility. Sexual acts that respect the ordination to procreation "say" with the language of the body, "I am willing to be a parent with you," and that is a statement that promises a lifetime commitment. Whatever their intentions, couples who engage in contraceptive sex are "saying" with their bodies that they want only a momentary union of pleasure. Those who are unmarried trivialize the meaning of sex and make it difficult to appreciate sex as an expression of commitment open to children.

Responsible couples engaging in noncontraceptive sex, on the other hand, express a willingness to share a lifetime union, since children help to create such a union. Sexual intercourse is meant to express and solidify this commitment to lifetime union that a couple has already made through their marriage vows. Indeed, a child is a living monument to the union of the couple, a person whose very being manifests the union of the mother and father, who continue to be united in the person of the child forevermore. Sexual acts that are open to children express more fully the lifetime commitment that marriage is.

Chemical contraceptives and the intrauterine device (IUD) sometimes work by preventing the embryonic human being from implanting in the mother's uterus. Thus using them is wrong for the same reason that abortion is wrong. But all contraceptives are anti-life and anti-love in important ways. Barriers are not appropriate between those who love each other. Chemical contraceptives also place a "barrier" between the sperm and the egg by preventing them from meeting. All contraceptives contradict the very ordination of the sexual act toward union of a husband's sperm and a wife's egg.

For those having sex, pregnancy is no accident; it is that toward which the act is ordained. Spouses, however, provide only the physical matter to create new human life; God himself supplies the new immortal soul (see *Evangelium Vitae*, 43). Thus spouses become cooperators with God in the creation of new human life. The ability to do this is of inestimable value and should not be treated as a physiological nuisance. The Catholic Church teaches that sex is sacred, children are sacred and the connection between sex and children is sacred; these are concepts that are hard to grasp in the modern world.

Question 26: Isn't Natural Family Planning just another form of contraception?

Briefly described, Natural Family Planning (NFP) works with the knowledge that women ovulate only once per cycle, that the egg lives in a woman's body for only twenty-four hours and that cervical mucus can keep sperm alive for up to five days.[9] Methods of NFP (not the old "rhythm method") help a woman identify the various signs of fertility, such as the appearance of fertile mucus, a rise in body temperature and physical changes in her cervix (not all methods use every sign). Generally, from seven to ten days of abstinence each cycle are required for those intending to avoid pregnancy. NFP methods also help identify the time of maximum fertility for those trying to achieve pregnancy.

Some people think the use of NFP and contraception are identical, since couples using both are intending to have sexual intercourse without getting pregnant. This intention in itself is not immoral; indeed, the Church does not teach that spouses must have as many children as their bodies and finances will bear. The Church also teaches that sexual intercourse is meant to advance marital union as well as bring forth children, and spouses who have good reasons for limiting their family size may use natural means of family limitation. Pope John Paul II spoke of "responsible parenthood," in which a couple uses practical wisdom, prayer and a spirit of generosity in determining how many children they should have (see *Familiaris Consortio,* 35).

Some Catholics believe that the Church permits the use of NFP only for reasons that verge on the truly desperate, such as a situation where a pregnancy would threaten a woman's life or a family is living in dire poverty. Magisterial documents, however, state that spouses may have physical, psychological, economic or social reasons for needing to limit family size, using several different adjectives to describe those reasons: One can have "just" reasons, "worthy" reasons, "defensible" reasons, "serious" reasons and "weighty" reasons.[10] In short, the Magisterium teaches that spouses must have unselfish reasons for using NFP and limiting their family size.

What is intrinsically immoral is the deliberate violation of one's fertility in order to manage family size. Contracepting couples make themselves infertile; NFP couples work with an infertility that is natural. Contraception treats fertility as a defect; NFP treats fertility as a gift to be treasured though perhaps not always opened. Contracepting couples do not give fully of themselves in the act of sexual intercourse; couples using NFP give all that they have to give during the times of infertility. Contraception is similar to telling a lie to get what one wants, whereas NFP is more akin to remaining silent when something should not be spoken.

Couples refrain from having sexual intercourse for all sorts of reasons, including such trivial ones as the desire to watch a TV show or the presence of a headache. An unselfish effort to manage family size seems like a more justifiable reason to abstain than these other reasons. For it is not wrong to limit family size if a couple is not being selfish. And they are doing nothing wrong by confining their spousal intercourse to the infertile periods, since there is nothing wrong in having intercourse during the infertile period.

Modern methods of NFP have enormous benefits. For instance, they cost nothing. The fact that they are chemical-free and have no bad physical side effects should make them particularly appealing to many people who prefer all things organic. And they are nearly as effective as the birth control pill.[11]

Perhaps most importantly, many people who have switched from contraception to NFP report that their marital relationship has been enhanced as a result. In fact, the vast majority of couples who use NFP have contracepted at one time, and nearly all of them testify that their marriages and their sex lives have improved once they abandoned contraception and embraced NFP. Most couples initially fear that the abstinence will be detrimental to intimacy, but after time they find an increase of intimacy.[12]

The wives in NFP marriages speak of feeling very respected by their husbands, who value their health. These women feel valued for much more than their sexual availability. Husbands speak of greater sexual self-mastery, greater love for their wives, greater appreciation of fertility and increased self-esteem. Both husbands and wives acknowledge that they communicate better and experience truer intimacy. Undoubtedly, these and other reasons explain why couples using NFP almost never divorce.[13]

Thus, in spite of or even because of periodic abstinence, NFP is overall very beneficial for relationships.[14]

Question 27: If contraception is intrinsically evil, why does the Church permit women to take contraceptives for medical purposes?

This question indicates a grasp of the principle that one can never do something morally wrong to achieve good (see question 9). The problem in understanding Church teaching might just be a problem with terminology. It is important to keep in mind that those who take hormones that cause infertility do not always engage in an act of contraception.

Sometimes women take the synthetic hormones that are in the pill to treat various conditions such as endometriosis and ovarian cysts. The same cluster of natural hormones that causes a woman to ovulate also provoke the growth of the endometrium and of ovarian cysts. The synthetic hormones in the contraceptive pill not only inhibit ovulation but also reduce endometriosis and the growth of ovarian cysts. The infertility that results from treatment of endometriosis or ovarian cysts is not something a woman directly intends: It is an indirect effect of treatment taken to attack other physical problems—problems, in fact, that impede her fertility. This is a legitimate application of the principle of double effect (question 9). A woman using synthetic hormones to treat various physical maladies is not contracepting. Note that she might not be sexually active. The sin of contraception always refers to an action that thwarts the procreative power of the sexual act. So it is wrong to say that women may morally "contracept" to treat various conditions; rather, to treat those conditions they can take hormones that will cause temporary infertility. In many cases what temporarily causes infertility in the long run restores fertility!

Let us note, however, that many faithful Catholic doctors think that there are very few occasions when it would be necessary for women to take infertility-causing hormones. In our culture many doctors prescribe the pill for all sorts of conditions that can be treated successfully by nonhormonal medicines and by lifestyle changes, including weight loss, proper nutrition and exercise. Women whose physicians recommend the pill for therapeutic reasons should attempt to discover if there are other viable treatments for their medical condition. They could consult an NFP-only physician—that is, a physician who does not prescribe contraceptives. They may be surprised to find that other treatment options are available.

Since the hormones in chemical contraceptives sometimes work by preventing implantation of the embryonic human being, some might ask if these hormones could cause an early-term abortion in a woman taking them for medical reasons. Wouldn't it be necessary for the couple to abstain completely to avoid the possibility of an early abortion?

Some physicians deny that prevention of implantation is an early-term abortion. They maintain that pregnancy does not begin until implantation. But since science has shown that human life begins at fertilization, the Church teaches that life deserves protection from that time. So it is right to be concerned not to do anything that would cause a baby to be aborted, even as a side effect of medication.

Sometimes it is permissible to do something that endangers the life or even causes the death of an embryonic human being as the result of some treatment (see question 16), but only when the good that is intended is proportionate to the danger to the child, such as saving the life of the mother.

Some have proposed that women using hormones causing infertility should use NFP and abstain during their infertile times. This cannot really be done, since a woman does not have the usual signs of fertility when she is taking these hormones. After all, the hormones are suppressing her fertility and thus the signs of fertility. Even use of the rhythm method would not work, since it simply would not be clear where a woman would be in her cycle.

Is complete abstinence the only moral option? Studies show that some infertility-causing hormones are virtually 100 percent effective in suppressing ovulation if they are taken at the same time every day and if the woman is not taking anything else that might interfere with the workings of those hormones. If a woman is dedicated to such a regimen, perhaps the level of risk of abortion is acceptable. There are very few actions in life that are without some element of risk, even risk to life. For instance, parents risk their children's lives and their own whenever they get in a car.

A woman, her husband and her doctor should do some serious research on how the hormones work in her body, specifically on how likely it is that she would ovulate and conceive. They might determine that the level of risk is acceptable.

Question 28: Is it moral for spouses to use a condom if one of them has the human immunodeficiency virus (HIV)?

The debate about the use of condoms to prevent HIV for married couples is ongoing, and as of yet, there has been no definitive statement on this matter from the Magisterium.

Some theologians and philosophers think that the principle of double effect (question 9) justifies the use of condoms by spouses to avoid transmitting HIV. They believe that the contraceptive effect of the condom is not what is primarily intended: What is intended is preventing transmission of a lethal disease. The argument is that the infertility caused by the condom should be considered a side effect, a double effect.

Most orthodox ethicists who have written on this topic consider all condom use by heterosexuals to be contraceptive and therefore immoral.[15]

Another consideration, which may be very pertinent to this question, is that common Catholic teaching holds that only completed acts of sexual intercourse are moral. Some theologians argue that since a male who uses a condom does not ejaculate in the female, the act of sexual intercourse is incomplete: No act of complete self-giving has taken place.

Couples who risk transmitting the HIV do not necessarily need to abstain for the rest of their marriage. In other questions we have noted that levels of risk factor into many decisions in life. Couples may be at a stage in their life where taking the risk of transmitting HIV may be acceptable to them, especially as treatments for HIV advance.

Some people maintain that the Church would be cruel not to permit a woman to ask or require that her husband use a condom if he has HIV and insists on having sex. They believe that this situation arises in many parts of the world and that the Church is contributing to millions of deaths because of her refusal to accept condom use as moral in these situations.

Of course, a wife could use a condom if her husband's pursuance of sexual intercourse truly constitutes rape and she has no moral means of resisting.[16] Suppose rape is not really what is going on but coercion: The husband threatens to leave his wife if she won't have sex with him, perhaps thereby casting her and her children into destitution.

Yet, approval of condom use may not be the sensible solution to tragic situations such as these. Rather, shouldn't the men behaving this way be encouraged to have greater respect for their wives? Some may say that such efforts at conversion or persuasion would not be practical, but is it practical to think that men in need of conversion will have a lifetime supply of condoms and will be responsible enough to use them? Is it moral to facilitate a situation where a husband continues to coerce his wife into having sex that may transmit a lethal disease?

Consider this analogy: We do not attempt to reduce drunk-driving accidents by urging drunks to drive carefully or to put on seatbelts. Rather we insist that they not drive at all. If sex has become an activity that may transmit a disease, it may be best to advise those in danger of transmitting or contracting the lethal disease to cease the activity if they consider the risk level unacceptable.

A related issue is the charge that the Catholic Church is responsible for the deaths of millions because it does not support the distribution of condoms to slow the spread of HIV.[17] Although some individuals have contracted HIV in other ways, the vast majority has contracted it through pre-marital sex, adultery, homosexual sex or needle sharing during illegal drug use. Is it likely that these people are not using condoms because the Catholic Church says they shouldn't? Is it remotely reasonable to think that the Church is the cause of death from HIV, rather than those who engage in immoral practices and those encouraging irresponsible sexuality, such as some people in the entertainment world?

If individuals were living by the Church's teaching on sexuality, the incidence of HIV would be negligible. In fact, the only country in Africa that has had success in reducing significantly the incidence of HIV transmission is Uganda, and its program places foremost emphasis on abstinence before marriage and fidelity within marriage.[18] Why should the Church abandon its message of chastity, a message that works, and embrace one that is less effective?

Question 29: Is it morally permissible to have sex with a contracepting spouse?

One should never use a contraceptive, even if one's spouse insists that one do so. But in some circumstances it is moral for a husband or wife to have sexual intercourse with a spouse who is contracepting.

A person who accepts the Church's teaching on contraception but whose spouse insists on using a contraceptive should attempt to persuade his or her spouse not to use the contraceptive, perhaps by supplying him or her with good books and CDs or trying to arrange a conversation with a persuasive individual. If efforts at persuasion fail, the Church teaches that the noncontracepting spouse is not necessarily sinning in having sex with the contracepting spouse if refusing intercourse would be significantly damaging to the relationship.[19]

The Church does not specify whether the kind of contraceptive a spouse is using makes a difference. Some faithful theologians argue that it would not be moral for a husband or wife to engage in sexual intercourse with a spouse using a condom. They argue that a condom prevents a completed act of sexual intercourse from taking place, since the condom not only prevents sperm from meeting an egg but also prevents deposit of semen in the vagina. They consider sexual intercourse with a condom to be no different from mutual masturbation or coitus interruptus. Yet other respected theologians claim that a condom does not prevent a completed act from taking place, and thus they would consider it moral for a spouse who opposes contraception to have sex with a spouse using a condom.

In question 27 we considered the morality of engaging in sexual intercourse when an abortifacient contraceptive is used. Here is yet another place where spouses must use the best judgment of their consciences. Recall that following one's conscience does not mean doing what one feels comfortable doing but trying to figure out what God would approve (see question 4).

Question 30: Is it moral to use contraceptives as post-rape treatment?

"The Ethical and Religious Directives for Health Care Services" of the USCCB permits victims of rape to take the hormones that are present in contraceptives to prevent a pregnancy if the prevention does not involve destroying the embryonic human being or preventing implantation.[20] Destruction of an embryonic human or preventing implantation is equivalent to abortion and thus immoral. If the treatment, however, works prior to the process of fertilization—by destroying or incapacitating the sperm or preventing ovulation, for instance—it is morally permissible.

Such treatments to prevent conception are permissible because they inhibit a part of the rapist (the sperm) from further advancement into the woman's body and prevent this part of the man from uniting with part of the woman's body (her egg). As such, this act differs morally from acts of contraceptive use during voluntary intercourse. It qualifies as an act of self-defense rather than an act of contraception.

One challenge in this process is to discern where a victim is in her ovulatory cycle. Post-rape anovulatory hormones can be used if it has been determined that the woman has not yet ovulated. It is moral for her to prevent ovulation or kill sperm to avoid being impregnated by the rapist, but it would not be moral for her to kill an embryonic human being to defend herself.

Post-rape treatment may not be wise, even when a woman is determined to be preovulatory. We must remember that conception after rape is rare.[21] For a pregnancy to occur, the raped woman must be at the fertile stage of her cycle and not contracepting, and the rapist must not be sterile. Even with all those elements in place, a pregnancy still may not happen. A woman may choose not to expose her body to all the bad side effects of massive doses of sterilizing hormones in an attempt to prevent something that is highly unlikely to happen.[22] She should consider the probable consequences of using the treatment or abstaining from treatment in coming to her decision.

Nor is it right to think that a pregnancy is the worst possible outcome of rape. Some women who have become pregnant through rape have carried the baby to term and found that their life-giving response to a violent event has helped them heal from the trauma.[23] Thus it is ethically permissible to prevent the rapist's sperm from uniting with the victim's egg, but the woman is under no obligation to undertake such prevention.

Question 31: Should parents have their daughters receive the vaccine for the human papillomavirus (HPV)?

The human papillomavirus (HPV) is usually transmitted through sexual intercourse. HPV is at present the most common sexually transmitted infection in the world, and several of its most common strains cause cervical cancer. The incidence of cervical cancer has decreased greatly in the United States since Pap smears became available. These allow early treatment both of the condition that is a precursor to cervical cancer and to cervical cancer itself. Nonetheless, not all women go for regular Pap smears, and not all Pap smears are conducted well, so some women still risk cervical cancer from HPV.

Efforts in various communities to make vaccinations for HPV mandatory for girls (the usual ages recommended are nine through eleven) argue that even those girls who abstain until marriage are at risk, since a future spouse may be infected or a girl may be a victim of rape at some time. Those who object to mandatory vaccination believe that there has not been sufficient testing to determine the long-term risks and effectiveness of the vaccine, that the billions necessary for universal vaccination would be better spent on ordinary health care for those who cannot afford it, and that it sends young girls the implicit message that we expect them to be sexually active.

Others believe that voluntary vaccination should be encouraged. They argue that studies of the vaccine are sufficient to determine that its risk is low, that the long-term savings from treatment of cancer would outweigh the costs and that parents are best able to determine what protection their daughters need and what message the vaccine would send in respect to immoral sexual behavior. The Catholic Medical Association, an organization faithful to the Magisterium, recommends wide distribution of the vaccine but maintains that it should not be mandatory and should require parental consent for minor girls.[24]

Question 32: Would it be moral to put a mentally handicapped woman on a contraceptive or have her sterilized if she is at risk of being sexually abused?

Some who advocate contraception or sterilization for the mentally handicapped believe that such individuals, since they are physically adults with adult physical desires, should not be denied sexual pleasure. Yet clearly sexual intercourse is much more than a source of physical pleasure; it is proper only for those who are emotionally mature and capable of a lifetime union open to children. We do not, for instance, allow very young teenagers to drive, although many have the physical capacity to do so.

Thus, to some extent, this question is not so different from the question of supervising anyone who is physically mature but not capable of making mature decisions, such as many teenagers. They are at risk not only of being sexually abused by others but also of their own poor decisions. Adults must try in every way to protect the immature from predators and from themselves.

Although great efforts should be made to protect disabled people from abuse of any kind, including sexual abuse, there are circumstances in which one might need to accept a risk of abuse. Parents sometimes must place their children in residential facilities, where unscrupulous caretakers could pose such a risk. Sexual intercourse in which true consent cannot be given because of the woman's mental defect constitutes a form of rape.

An office of the Vatican in the late 1950s was asked if it would be moral for some nuns in the Congo who believed they were in grave danger of being raped to use contraceptives, and the office responded in the affirmative.[25] The discussion in question 30 might apply here. Contraception in such cases would not be a violation of the meaning of a voluntary act of sexual intercourse but rather a means of self-defense. Some theologians who accept the teaching of the Magisterium have argued that even sterilization is permissible in order to prevent a pregnancy from an unjust act of sexual intercourse.[26]

Yet we must consider whether the risks of pregnancy are proportionate to other risks involved. Even otherwise responsible caretakers who know that a woman is on a contraceptive or sterilized may be less vigilant in supervising her. Even worse, evil caretakers may be more likely to take advantage of such a woman. The woman also would risk all the bad physical side effects that come with chemical contraceptives.

This is another question that theologians and philosophers faithful to the teaching of the Church continue to debate. People confronting this issue must seek wise counsel, pray and trust the Lord for guidance.

Question 33: Is it morally permissible for a woman to be sterilized if her uterus is so damaged that she could not get through a pregnancy safely?

If a woman's uterus is so unhealthy that it poses a threat to her well-being, it would be moral for her to have the uterus removed—that is, to get a hysterectomy. It is moral to remove organs and body parts that pose threat to an individual's well-being; for example, gangrenous limbs may be removed.

Sometimes, however, the uterus is not a threat to a woman's health when she is not pregnant but may become a threat were she to become pregnant. For instance, a woman may have scar tissue on her uterus that might cause the uterus to rupture as it expands in pregnancy, thus causing potentially life-threatening hemorrhaging. Many doctors recommend that such women get hysterectomies in order to make a future pregnancy impossible.

Some doctors recommend not a full hysterectomy to prevent pregnancy but what is called a "uterine isolation." This procedure is identical to a tubal ligation: A woman has her fallopian tubes "tied," thus isolating the uterus from the fallopian tubes.

The Church, through a declaration by the Congregation of the Doctrine of the Faith, has declared that hysterectomies to prevent future pregnancies and "uterine isolations" are not morally permissible.[27] Both procedures involve the direct intent to prevent a pregnancy, and that is a contraceptive or sterilizing intent. The Church teaches that acts that directly cause sexual acts to be infertile are intrinsically wrong.

Couples facing serious medical situations of this type would want to learn a very reliable method of Natural Family Planning and follow it with due diligence.

Question 34: Are couples who have been sterilized morally obliged to get a reversal?

Sterilized couples have attempted to render themselves permanently infertile. Some repent of that action. Is it possible for them truly to have repented of their sterilization if they do not get a reversal—that is, if they continue to "reap the benefits" of their sterilization: "pregnancy-free" sex?

First, it is important to realize that "pregnancy-free sex" is not, objectively speaking, a benefit. Those who truly have repented of their sterilization profoundly regret that they have attempted to thwart their fertility permanently. They may not desire more children, but nonetheless, true repentance would involve regret that they have rejected the procreative power of the sexual act. They realize that their "acts of complete self-giving" are not as complete as they should be.

Normally sinners should attempt to repair the damage done by their sins. Liars generally should tell the truth to those to whom they have lied; thieves should return stolen goods. Couples who have had a reversal of their sterilization speak of the profound graces that the reversal brings to their marriage.[28]

If getting a reversal could be done without undue physical and financial burdens, some theologians argue that it would be obligatory for a couple to seek one. But currently reversal procedures can be financially prohibitive. For some the level of risk involved in the surgery, while small, may not be proportionate to the good sought.

If a reversal is prohibitive, must a couple practice NFP as a means of rectifying their situation? A woman who has had a tubal ligation will ovulate and have signs of fertility; it would be possible for her and her husband to use NFP as a way of pursuing the life they likely would lead were they not sterilized. The Church has no explicit teaching on this matter. Orthodox Catholic thinkers disagree on the correct answer.

John Kippley, founder of the Couple to Couple League, argues that it is "psychologically impossible for a couple to enjoy sterilized sexual relations during the fertile time without reaffirming a contraceptive will."[29] He maintains that couples who have been sterilized must get a reversal if possible.

Others argue that some couples truly regret the impossibility of future pregnancies even though they may have good reasons for avoiding them. The regret these couples experience may constitute a kind of penance. In their case sterility becomes equivalent to that of couples who are infertile through no fault of their own.

Some couples may choose to use NFP as a penance or to help themselves be attentive to the procreative power of sexual intercourse, but it is not a moral necessity that all sterilized couples do so. After all, many sinners to some extent get to "enjoy the fruits" of their sin even after repentance. Women who have children out of wedlock or who have children through in vitro fertilization are not required to give up their children as a penance for their wrongdoing. Certainly sinners must fully repent of their actions, but they do not *always* need to "return the goods" they have received.

CHAPTER FIVE

End-of-Life Issues

Question 35: What is euthanasia?

The term *euthanasia* literally means "good death," but it has largely come to mean "mercy killing." *Mercy* here refers to alleviating suffering. The thought is that it would be merciful to kill those who would prefer to die rather than endure a state of physical or mental incapacity.

The call to legalize euthanasia is a call to legalize practices that intentionally kill innocent human beings. The Congregation for the Doctrine of the Faith has stated: "By euthanasia is understood an action or an omission which of itself or by intention causes death, in order that all suffering may in this way be eliminated. Euthanasia's terms of reference, therefore, are to be found in the intention of the will and in the methods used."[1]

Direct euthanasia refers to killing a patient intentionally as a means or as an end. Direct euthanasia can be done by either commission or omission. In euthanasia by commission, or active euthanasia, someone takes an active measure, such as lethal injection, to kill a patient. In euthanasia by omission, or passive euthanasia, someone responsible for providing care omits morally obligatory treatment in order to kill the patient. (In question 37 we will explain when it is morally permissible to withhold or stop treatment and simply let the dying process take over.) The

Church reserves the term *euthanasia* for intentional killing, whether by commission or omission; thus it teaches that both active and passive euthanasia are morally wrong.

Voluntary euthanasia refers to a situation in which a patient asks to be killed; *nonvoluntary euthanasia* refers to a situation in which a patient has not indicated whether or not he or she desires to be killed; and *involuntary euthanasia* refers to a situation in which a patient is killed against his or her will.

Almost everyone agrees that killing an innocent person against that person's will is wrong, whether one does it by directly killing the person or by allowing a person to die when one could save that person with a reasonable amount of effort. For instance, there is no moral difference between directly drowning someone (say, holding his or her head underwater) and standing by and letting someone drown when one easily could rescue the person. Neither is there a moral difference between giving someone a lethal injection and refusing reasonable care, such as not putting a tourniquet on someone who is bleeding profusely in order to kill him.

It is difficult in our culture to explain why it is not morally permissible to kill someone who wants to die, unless one understands the true value of human life and our responsibilities to each patient no matter how ill (see questions 38 and 41). It is also difficult sometimes to determine the difference between the morally impermissible act of passive euthanasia, which involves withholding morally obligatory treatment with the intention that someone die, and the morally permissible act of withholding optional treatment even though death is foreseen. We shall address this issue in the section on ordinary and extraordinary means (question 40).

Question 36: Is there an ethical difference between *active* euthanasia (intending the death of the patient by some act) and *passive* euthanasia (intending the death of the patient by some omission)?

In terms of morality, there is no essential moral difference between passive and active euthanasia, since both involve the intention to kill an innocent person, either by commission or by omission. Consider two examples. Suppose Joe and Burt both want their wives to die so that they can collect insurance money. Following dinner, Joe strangles his wife to death. Burt also plans to strangle his wife after dinner, but after her first bite of fish, she begins to choke on a fishbone. Although Burt knows the Heimlich maneuver and easily could save her, he simply watches as she struggles for breath and dies.

Is there an important difference between Joe's action and Burt's inaction? Joe performed an action intending to kill; Burt by omitting an action intended to kill. They both did wrong; they both killed intentionally.

In active euthanasia an action is done with the intention of killing, such as lethally injecting a patient. In passive euthanasia someone does not perform a life-saving action that one should, such as doing the Heimlich maneuver in the example above. Both the act and the omission are means of killing an innocent person, and both are wrong.

Question 37: Is it always wrong to let someone die?

Not necessarily. "Letting someone die" means allowing someone who is dying from some underlying condition to die. One foresees that the individual will die but decides not to take means to prolong the dying person's life. Letting someone die is morally permissible when one does not intend to bring about the patient's death and when one does not withhold some ordinary, obligatory treatment (see question 40).

To understand the distinction between passive euthanasia on the one hand and the morally permissible act of letting someone die on the other, we must understand the importance of the distinction between intending an effect and merely foreseeing that some effect will result without intending it. Common sense holds that there is an important moral difference between the two.

Imagine two dentists, Emma and Frank, who are seeing patients with a similar dental condition. Emma foresees that the needed tooth extraction will cause pain but knows that if the tooth is not extracted, the patient will suffer even more in the future. Frank, on the other hand, enjoys seeing his patients writhe in pain and so makes sure that he removes the tooth in the most painful manner possible. Emma foresees but does not intend pain, while Frank intends the pain. There is a world of moral difference between them.

To articulate the principle at issue, it is wrong to intend an evil effect—such as pain or death—for the sake of inflicting harm, whereas at times it is moral to perform some action or omit some action although one foresees that an evil effect will result. In these latter instances the evil must not be intended. Applying this to the issue at hand leads to the distinction between euthanasia (intending to kill the innocent) and letting someone die.

An extremely important factor in trying to understand the moral legitimacy of letting someone die is that death, though not in itself good, can lead to good things. For instance, death frees some people from terrible pain and suffering. For martyrs death is a part of their glory. What is key for our consideration is that Catholics understand death to be a point of passage to eternal life. We are not to hasten our death, but we are to accept it as a natural part of the human condition.

There are times when, in fact, attempting to prolong one's life would be immoral. For example, denying one's faith to save one's life is wrong, and paying enormous sums of money to pursue untested treatments may be an immoral use of funds. When a medical treatment promises little benefit but great burden, the treatment need not be administered, even if it is foreseen that omitting it leads to someone's death.

Understanding when it is moral to let someone die requires explanation of the difference between ordinary treatment, which we are obliged to provide a dying patient, and extraordinary treatment, which is optional. It is moral to refuse extraordinary treatment (see question 40).

Question 38: Is life always a good, even when it involves great suffering?

Life is intrinsically good for every person (see questions 1 and 2), even when we encounter intense physical, psychological or spiritual suffering. We must remember that sometimes good things make evil possible, and sometimes evil makes good possible (see question 7 for an explanation of the word *evil*). For instance, the good of eyesight makes possible the evil of painful sun glare. The evil of harming another person makes possible the goods of repentance, forgiveness and reconciliation.

The fact that an evil may come from a good and a good may come from an evil, however, does not mean that evil *becomes* good or good *becomes* evil. Good is good and evil is evil, even in cases where they are intertwined.

If someone is kidnapped and forced to live on bread and water without communicating with another person for a year, he or she may emerge from this captivity more compassionate, thoughtful and dedicated to the eradication of injustice. But none of that changes the fact that kidnapping the individual was wrong, a moral evil.

Conversely, the good of having eyesight and intelligence may lead to the evil of seeing for oneself an ugly truth that causes deep emotional pain. But although we may not like what we see or come to know, eyesight and intelligence are goods for human beings, and to lack them is an evil.

Suffering terrible pain is not in itself a good, but it does not follow from this that those who suffer greatly have "wrongful life" or have lost their dignity. In a culture that considers pleasure to be the number one priority, to be in pain—to be debilitated or depressed or psychologically disturbed, indeed, to be suffering in any way—can seem to rob a person of dignity. The most fundamental form of dignity, however, is intrinsic to the human person and cannot be lost. Every human being possesses this dignity from the very beginning of life, through all stages of life and until death, regardless of ability or disability.

Fortunately, at least in developed countries, for the most part it is possible to control physical pain. Indeed, we have never in human history been so able to treat and alleviate physical pain, although not all physicians may be as informed about pain management as they should be. Moreover, although pain management can relieve physical suffering, sometimes it results in a patient's loss of consciousness. Psychological pain and spiritual pain are really of no less concern than physical pain. We have made great progress in developing drugs and therapy that help alleviate even these kinds of suffering.

Relieving the physical, psychological and spiritual pain of others is an extremely important human challenge. But we should strive to eliminate these problems through all feasible means rather than resort to killing persons suffering from them.

Nonetheless, we should not lose sight of the fact that great good can and does come from suffering (see question 3). In fact, we can advance our human dignity through suffering. Those who continue to live in accord with the truth and do not circumvent the moral law in seeking alleviation of their troubles grow in virtue. Many have found meaning in a life of suffering—a life perhaps marked with severe disabilities, imprisonment and pain. These people focus on serving God and neighbor heroically despite and through their suffering. Some find through suffering a reason to deepen their spiritual lives, to strengthen love relationships and to reconcile damaged relationships. And for

Christians, all suffering is an opportunity to ponder more deeply the great gift that Christ gave us in his passion. He refused to do anything immoral to escape an agonizing death. We need to pray for the strength to witness to the truth to the last.

The dying process itself often entails considerable suffering—for the patient certainly and also for the patient's loved ones. Yet those who care for the dying often speak of the great peace that patients and their loved ones gain through dealing with the dying process as an opportunity for spiritual growth. Indeed, many dying individuals experience a profound sense of God's love for them, a sense that he is waiting for them.

Finally, the suffering that our loved ones undergo sometimes makes it easier for us to let them go.

Question 39: What is the Christian view of the relationship of the soul to the body, and how does it influence the moral evaluation of end-of-life treatments?

What is the relationship of the body and the soul? What am I really, and what are you?

Some argue that we are just minds that occupy bodies as vehicles for the mind, much like an engine in a car. They think that who we are is simply our minds, our consciousness and our thoughts. Another view is that we are just matter, and there is no spiritual element to us at all.

A third view—that of many philosophers and of the Church—is that we are a unity of body and mind: the body is the matter, and the soul is its vivifying "form." We are bodily spirits; spiritual bodies; unions of body and soul, matter and mind.

Let us first address the view that we are simply matter.

The great ancient pre-Christian philosophers, such as Plato and Aristotle, argued that we cannot understand man unless we acknowledge that there is a spiritual element in us. That spiritual element they called the soul. The soul is the principle of life. What necessitates its being spiritual is that, being rational, it is able to understand all things. A material soul could not understand all things, since matter is limited.

A philosophical analysis of human experience and our experience of knowing (and even our emotional lives) indicate that we could not be simply matter alone. For instance, when we know something, we have in some sense "united" with the thing we are knowing. But these things do not exist in our minds in a material way. For instance, when someone knows a human being, there is not a tiny human being in his or her brain. Our spiritual minds, with the help of the senses, grasp all the material features of a thing and its essence as well; if our minds were material they could not do this amazing task.

Ancient philosophers also argued that the human soul is immortal because only material things are corruptible, so since the human soul is spiritual—that is, immaterial—it is incorruptible. Christians have an additional reason for believing in the existence and immortality of the soul (and body): Christ himself assured us that we are destined for eternal life. So both philosophy and faith reject the claim that human beings are only matter.

Let us next examine the view that human beings are merely minds and that the body is not an essential part of human identity. Those who hold this view say that bodies, biological lives, are merely what enable thinking beings to exist. Some religious thinkers who hold this view believe that it is our souls that make us who we are, and our souls are understood to be our minds. In this view, when consciousness is no longer possible, the *patient* has died, and the soul is no longer present. The person someone once was is no longer there. The body that the soul inhabited may continue to exist, just like a car whose battery has died, but since the conscious "I" is no longer in existence, there is nothing of value remaining.

This view contradicts the gospel and reason itself. In his encyclical *Veritatis Splendor,* Pope John Paul II wrote:

> This moral theory does not correspond to the truth about man and his freedom. It contradicts the *Church's teachings on the unity of the human person....* The spiritual and immortal soul is the principle of unity of the human being, whereby it exists as a whole—*corpore et anima unus* [one in body and soul]—as a person. These definitions...point out that the body, which has been promised the resurrection, will also share in glory. (48)[2]

In every human person, body and soul form the unity that is that person. The body alone is not the person; the soul alone is not the person. In *Evangelium Vitae* Pope John Paul II wrote of "the inseparable connection between the person, his life and his bodiliness" (81).

In other words, our body, our biological life, is an essential aspect of who we are, not merely something that we use or occupy like a car or a suit of clothing.

Philosophically speaking, to claim that you and I are merely our minds, our consciousness or memories and that our bodies are not an essential part of who we are makes it difficult to explain commonsense intuitions.[3] If someone hits another in the stomach, he has really hit that person, not merely something that the person is only "inhabiting," "occupying" or "using." A rapist harms the *woman* whom he attacks, not merely a body that she makes use of. The rape of an unconscious person or someone in a persistent vegetative state would still be the rape of a person.

Therefore, we *are* our *bodies*, though not just bodies alone. We are "ensouled" bodies, or bodily spirits. The body alone is not us; the soul alone is not us; rather we are body *and* soul. Our biological life is more than a good simply to be used.

Theologically speaking, this truth is important, for it highlights the radical nature of the Incarnation: When Jesus, the Second Person of the Trinity, became embodied, he did not only "appear" to have a body; he truly took on human flesh inside Mary.

Moreover, the natural unity of human body and soul explains the need for the resurrection of the body at the Last Day, when all the dead will be reunited with their bodies: The whole person, body and soul, will be immortal, not just the soul. This fact of the unity of body and soul also reinforces the understanding that unconscious individuals are not "soulless." The soul is what gives the body life, thus as long as a human body is living, it still possesses a soul; there is still a person present.

This fact bears on end-of-life issues. Since we are intrinsically valuable, our lives are also intrinsically valuable. It is this value that is not properly respected in the killing of innocent people, whether in murder or in suicide or in euthanasia. Even those who do not have a good "quality" of life still possess life, a good of inestimable value.

Some people ask, "Why can't we do anything we want with our bodies?" The basic reasons are that our bodies are gifts from God and that morality requires that we should seek not simply whatever we want but rather what God wants. Love of God calls us to put our entire selves, both body and spirit, in service to God and other people. Killing innocent human beings, ourselves or others, contradicts this great calling.

Catholics believe that our lives do not belong to us; rather they belong to God. Indeed, through baptism a person is made the temple of the Holy Spirit and deserves the full reverence such a temple demands.

Question 40: What is the difference between ordinary means and extraordinary means of preserving life?

Although euthanasia (active or passive) is always wrong, since it involves the intentional killing of an innocent human being, it is not always wrong to cease treatments or not to begin treatments when someone is dying. This is true even if we anticipate that stopping a treatment or omitting a treatment will shorten the person's life. As we noted in question 37, letting someone die is sometimes a moral choice.

The distinction between ordinary and extraordinary means helps to determine which treatments are obligatory (ordinary means) and which treatments are not obligatory but are optional (extraordinary means). The terms themselves are somewhat misleading, insofar as *ordinary* and *extraordinary* normally have to do with how common something is or how frequently it is used. Sometimes what is *medically* ordinary (that is, often used) may be morally optional and thus extraordinary in the moral sense. Similarly, sometimes what is *medically* extraordinary (that is, rarely used) may be morally obligatory and thus is called "ordinary" in moral judgments.

In the sense in which Catholic tradition uses these terms, *ordinary means* refers to treatments that are more beneficial than burdensome to the patient and others, while *extraordinary means* refers to treatments in which the benefits do not correspond to the burdens of treatment. As we shall see, "burdens" can include cost and inconvenience as well as pain and discomfort. Sometimes this same distinction is referred to by other names, such as "proportionate" and "disproportionate" means of preserving life.

Whatever terminology is employed, the important point is that although *human life* is always a good, in a particular situation a *medical treatment* may be more burdensome than beneficial. Some treatments are not worth pursuing because of the burdens they entail and the meager benefits they are expected to produce. Such treatments qualify as "extraordinary means." We have no obligations to begin or continue them, even if this means that we will die. Again, we are speaking here of some treatments as being burdensome, not of lives as being burdensome or not worth living.

When is a medical treatment beneficial and therefore obligatory? To the degree that a treatment prolongs life, cures, restores function, relieves symptoms, alleviates pain and engenders physical or psychological well-being, to that degree a treatment is beneficial. But again, simply being beneficial is not enough to make a treatment mandatory: The benefits must outweigh the burdens.

What makes a treatment burdensome? Some treatments are financially costly, psychologically repugnant, physically painful or discomforting, unlikely to succeed, unlikely to provide great benefit, experimental or difficult to administer. They may also have detrimental side effects.

In determining whether or not a given procedure should be begun or continued, patients and physicians must assess the likely benefits and burdens of the procedure for a particular patient. The same treatment—for instance, a heart transplant—may be obligatory for one patient (an otherwise healthy twenty-year-old, for example) and not obligatory for another patient (such as a cancer-ridden ninety-year-old). Again, what is in question is whether the *procedure* is worthwhile, not whether the *person's life* is worthwhile.

If a given treatment is unduly burdensome for a particular patient, the treatment is extraordinary for that patient, and the patient may refuse to begin or continue it. The decision to refuse extraordinary treatment does not constitute suicide, even though death may result from the refusal.

If the benefits of a treatment outweigh the burdens of the treatment, such treatment is ordinary and obligatory. A patient's refusal of ordinary treatment amounts to suicide, and denying a patient such treatment amounts to killing that patient.

Although the Catholic tradition teaches absolutely that innocent life must be protected from intentional harm, at the same time it recognizes that patients are not obliged to pursue all treatments, even life-preserving treatments.

Again, when in doubt, those who make decisions about medical care must consider prayerfully the balance of burden and benefit for a particular patient.

Question 41: Should food and water be provided for patients in a persistent vegetative state?

For many years Catholic theologians have debated about the proper care for patients in a persistent vegetative state (PVS). These patients are also sometimes, and perhaps more properly, referred to as patients with persistent cognitive-affective deprivation. They no longer have self-awareness; they no longer are able to communicate or to reason. They may continue to live for a very long time in this state. Unfortunately, recovery of any ability to think or exercise free will is extremely rare. Should PVS patients receive artificial nutrition and hydration, even if regaining consciousness is extremely unlikely?

As we noted in question 39, some people have asserted that such human beings are really dead, though their bodies continue to live. According to this view, a person has ceased to exist when he or she can no longer think and is unlikely to regain that ability. Others argue that since PVS patients do not have a high quality of life, their lives are not worth living.

As we saw in questions 3 and 39, the Catholic Church holds that although some human beings cannot exercise even the most minimal of human powers, they are still fully human and deserve the full respect due human persons. In 2004 Pope John Paul II addressed this matter in a papal allocution to participants at an academic conference devoted to studying the provision of artificial nutrition and hydration (ANH) to a PVS patient. "I feel the duty to reaffirm strongly," the pope said, "that the intrinsic value and personal dignity of every human being do not change, no matter what the concrete circumstances of his or her life. *A man, even if seriously ill or disabled in the exercise of his highest functions, is and always will be a man*, and he will never become a 'vegetable' or an 'animal.'"[4] A human being is always a person, a being with moral worth, even when deprived of cognitive and affective function.

Theologians at the conference asked a second question: "Does food and water, given for example by means of tubes, constitute extraordinary means, a medical treatment, that need not be given to a PVS patient?" Pope John Paul II answered:

> I should like particularly to underline how the administration of water and food, even when provided by artificial means, always represents a *natural means* of preserving life, not a *medical act*. Its use, furthermore, should be considered, in principle, *ordinary* and *proportionate*, and as such morally obligatory, insofar as and until it is seen to have attained its proper finality, which in the present case consists in providing nourishment to the patient and alleviation of his suffering.[5]

The phrase "insofar as and until it is seen to have attained its proper finality" is important. The pope is not claiming that food and water must be given in all circumstances whatsoever. If a patient cannot assimilate food and water, then there is no obligation to administer them. Sometimes when patients are imminently dying, they can no longer digest food and water. Their systems simply cannot take in the nutrients and make use of them. There is no need to provide food and water for such patients.

Yet PVS patients are not normally in that condition; as mentioned, they often can live for decades with the aid of ANH and simple medical care. In these instances ANH is achieving its goal of providing ordinary care. Thus, as Pope John Paul II teaches, in such situations provision of food and water, even by artificial means such as tubes, is obligatory.

This teaching poses challenges for some Catholic hospitals and individuals. Many Catholic hospitals in recent years have withdrawn ANH from PVS patients, believing that the death that inevitably follows is from underlying causes rather than from the lack of hydration. They have considered ANH to be extraordinary care for such patients. The statement by Pope John Paul II unambiguously asserts that ANH is not extraordinary care for those in a PVS; indeed, he claims it is not *treatment* at all but ordinary *care* and thus always obligatory. Omitting ANH would be euthanasia by omission.

Some hospitals and individuals believe that they do not need to abide by this teaching because it is relatively new and is not taught with the highest degree of Church authority (see question 5). But shouldn't Catholic hospitals abide by Church teaching even if it is not taught with the highest authority? Theologians may call for further refinement of the teaching through proper channels, and private individuals may exercise their freedom of conscience in terms of matters not bindingly taught (see questions 4 and 5), but institutions representing the Church should act in accordance with the guidance the Church gives.

The Holy Father recognizes that care for PVS patients may be particularly demanding. The moral obligation of care in such situations extends beyond PVS patients to the families supporting them. "It is necessary, above all," the pope said, *"to support those families* who have had one of their loved ones struck down by this terrible clinical condition. They cannot be left alone with their heavy human, psychological and financial burden."[6]

Question 42: How should one respond to the request "Will you help me die?"

No one wants to die simply in order to die; those who wish to die wish to escape some difficulty of life, not life itself. Disputes arise about what to do when a patient, apparently of sound mind but suffering from some terrible condition, requests that a physician do something to help bring about death.

Wanting to die can be an understandable response to the condition in which one finds oneself. In fact, sometimes it is right to pray that an individual near death and in great suffering will die, since the Christian understands death to be a transition to the next life. For those in a state of grace it is a "homecoming" to the mansions of our loving God. But since God is the author of life and death, it is wrong for us to decide when we die.

Again, usually individuals asking for help in dying do not desire death; rather they fear or loathe the pain, debilitating dependence upon others or the humiliations that come with impaired abilities. Sometimes requests for assistance in committing suicide abate once patients receive sufficient pain management (which modern medicine nearly always can provide) or when they receive needed antidepressants.

But sometimes careful discernment is needed to determine what really lies behind the desire for death. When someone asks for physician-assisted suicide or euthanasia, what is he or she really asking for? Dr. Philip Muskin, of the Psychiatry Department at Columbia University, wrote an important article about this question called "The Request to Die" for the *Journal of the American Medical Association*.[7] He notes that such requests are relatively rare and usually not a result of pain alone. Muskin notes that the question "Will you help me end my life?" can mean any one or combination of the following questions:

Am I loved and wanted? A patient requesting help in dying may be asking for affirmation that, despite illness, others really do care for him or her and do not simply want him or her "out of the way." The patient may be asking for a *reason* to live.

What can I do? Muskin notes that the request to die can be an effort to reestablish control and choice over life. People want to be free to decide their destiny. But there is no authentic freedom in choosing an evil—and suicide is an evil. Authentic freedom consists in choosing the good.

A patient can control his or her destiny without choosing to die. Not choosing to die also expresses control, ongoing control. Indeed, a patient controls his or her own destiny in terms of how to handle the dying process. It can become a time for reconciliation, for honest self-reflection on life and for celebrating all that has come before.

Who am I? Dr. Muskin notes that some patients experience a "split self" and wish to kill off the "unhealthy self." Although such desire to escape is not atypical, the desire is ultimately mere fantasy, for during life there is no human "self" apart from the human body. It is important for people to realize that they have dignity even when their bodies fail them. Our human dignity does not rest on the frail foundation of our bodily health but in our very nature as children of God.

Where is justice? Often suicidal people wish to take revenge on others, even on God. The question of evil is a profound one. How can there be such great suffering in the world? Particularly, how can a loving and all-powerful God allow this? (See question 3.)

These questions are important, but committing suicide does not answer them. Indeed, killing oneself foregoes the possibility of grappling with the problem.

Where is hope? It is current medical practice to give very "realistic" assessments of a patient's life expectancy. Some patients then experience hopelessness, and so they request physician assistance in suicide. Again, the question is a good one. At times there may be virtually no chance— outside of miraculous intervention—for a person to recover from disease.

For Christians, however, hope can remain even in such dire circumstances. True hope, a theological virtue, resides in the trust that God will bring salvation and eternal happiness to us. This hope can always exist, even in the final stages of life. Conversely, true hope can be absent even in those who are perfectly healthy.

Can I be forgiven? Finally, Dr. Muskin notes that some patients request help in dying because of their desire to punish themselves (as penance for sin) and atone for guilt caused by their personal wrongdoing or failure to please (through being cured) doctors and loved ones. Although self-denial and voluntary mortification have a place in the pursuit of virtue, killing oneself is a different matter entirely.

Again, the question at heart is a good one, but the answer is not suicide. Catholics find the answer for the very real problem of guilt in the sacrament of reconciliation, wherein they receive forgiveness for their sins.

Is it possible that a patient who requests help in dying really does desire to die and is not running from other problems? Certainly. But that is not a request we should grant. We deny many requests, such as requests for drugs to feed an addiction. True love and concern for others consists in doing good for them, not simply granting any requests they make.

Since life is always a good, to intentionally kill another is to inflict a grave, irreversible injury. If a patient asks for help in killing him or herself, true help is desperately needed. Such individuals may need psychiatric, medical and spiritual help from highly trained professionals. True friends will get them help from such sources.

Question 43: Are advance directives helpful?

Advance directives can be very helpful for patients, their physicians and their families, since such directives provide guidance for the proxy decision maker and physician should a patient become incapacitated. The complexity of medical care and diversity of values make it in general unwise for patients simply to allow their physicians *carte blanche* on what is the best medical care for them in all situations.

Advance directives require that individuals think through a variety of possible medical situations and consider what sort of care they would desire in each. For example, patients beginning to suffer from Alzheimer's could direct that once the disease is far progressed, they do not want to be hospitalized but would rather spend their remaining days being cared for at home. An advance directive can ensure that the health care provided corresponds with the patient's religious and ethical beliefs when the patient is no longer able to speak for himself or herself.

Advance directives differ from living wills in that living wills often are considered to be absolutely binding, whereas advance directives are not. Sometimes patients with living wills might not get proper care because they have not anticipated what situations they might meet and thus have not provided directives for those situations. For instance, a flat refusal of any recourse to a ventilator (with the intention of preventing prolonged dependence on a ventilator) might have the unforeseen consequence of preventing recourse to a ventilator for a short time when it would help lead to full recovery.

In addition to providing advance directives, a patient should give durable power of attorney to a proxy decision maker. The proxy decision maker should be someone who understands well the values of the patient and who can be trusted to have health care decisions made in accordance with them. Often a family member or close friend is a good choice for a proxy.

Various organizations provide advance directive forms that help patients anticipate decisions that may need to be made in the future.[8] It is wise to talk over these directives not only with one's proxy decision maker but also with family members and one's physician. Different states have different policies on the legal force of advance directives. Individuals and their proxies should periodically review directives to clarify what values should drive any medical decision.

Question 44: Why does the determination of death matter?

The determination of death matters for a number of reasons. First, while it is moral to take organs from a dead body to help a living person, it is not moral to take organs from one living person to give them to another, if one thereby mutilates or causes the death of the donor. On the other hand, removing organs from the dead body of a person who agreed to be an organ donor is not mutilation.

In addition, a determination of death allows for just allocation of resources; hospital staff can cease allocating valuable resources to the deceased and channel them to others in need.

The determination of death also has various important religious, social and legal consequences.

A priest will not administer the anointing of the sick nor give Holy Communion to a dead person. Death routinely requires a funeral and burial; for those who are married, it means the end of the marriage and usually initiates a period of grieving for family and friends.

The death of a person often creates legal responsibilities for others. The death of a person may require a change in leadership of a company or be relevant for insurance claims.

Question 45: What is "brain death"? Does the Church approve of using neurological criteria to determine death?

For centuries doctors determined that patients were dead when for a certain period of time their hearts stopped beating and they no longer were able to breathe. These criteria served sufficiently to determine that an individual was dead until cardiopulmonary bypass machines enabled people to continue to live after their hearts stopped beating spontaneously and when they could no longer breathe on their own.

In addition, desire for organ transplants fueled a reconsideration of the criteria for death. Organs from cadavers declared dead by cardiopulmonary criteria have been deprived of oxygen for some time and are not suitable for transplanting. Physicians needed a way to obtain organs that had not begun to deteriorate. They began to argue that when the brain is "dead," the patient is dead, since they understood the brain to be the integrating organ of the body. The body parts of a person declared brain dead are generally suitable for transplanting since machines have been keeping them oxygenated.

First proposed by a committee at the Harvard School of Medicine in 1968, brain death—or the determination of death by neurological criteria—became widely accepted. In the United States whole brain death is a legally governing standard of death.

"Brain death" does not primarily mean the patient's brain is dead; rather, it means that the patient has been declared dead using criteria related to the functioning of the brain. In whole brain death the entire brain has ceased functioning as a unit, although individual cells or pockets of cells may still be living.

In the Catholic tradition, no one disagrees that when the soul has left the body, it is moral to discontinue all life support equipment, since there is no human life there to continue to support. Moreover, everyone also agrees that it is permissible to take organs from someone who is dead. There is a debate, however, about whether or not neurological criteria—brain death criteria—are sufficient to determine that a patient has truly died, that the soul is no longer united with the body.

To speak in religious or philosophical terms, brain death advocates would be committed to the principle that the soul makes use of the brain to integrate the body. In their view, when the brain as a whole ceases to function, the soul has lost its means of connection to the body and thus can no longer function as the integrative principle of the body. In other words, the soul leaves the body of someone whose brain is no longer functioning as a whole, and therefore the person is dead.

Those who accept brain death criteria, at least in the Catholic tradition, are not maintaining that the *body* is alive even though the *person* is dead. Rather, they mean that although *parts* of the body are still functioning with the assistance of medical machinery, the entire organism no longer operates as an integrated *whole* because of some internal integrating principle. They maintain that machines are keeping the *body functioning;* they are not keeping the whole human person alive. Brain death advocates consider the brain dead person to be just as dead as the person declared dead by cardiopulmonary criteria: the *parts* are living, not the *whole*.

The vast majority of physicians, including Catholic physicians, accept brain death criteria. Yet a significant number of physicians—both secular and Christian—have argued that brain dead people are not really dead. They argue that even though the brain is no longer integrating the body, the body is still operating as an integrated whole. They argue that the soul does not need the brain to integrate the body. Therefore the soul still is animating the body and still is exercising its integrative power.

Critics of brain death criteria point out that there are some things dead bodies cannot do that brain dead people have done. In one famous case a boy, called "TK" to protect his privacy, went through puberty and continued to live more than a decade after being diagnosed as brain dead.[9] Women declared brain dead have delivered babies. Those who qualify as brain dead can eliminate bodily waste, fight off infections, grow toward maturity, gestate a fetus and maintain body temperature. Their wounds can heal. Such characteristics, argue critics, indicate that brain death does not bring a loss of integrative unity.

These critics further argue that while the brain facilitates and refines various subsystems of the body, it does not actually provide the body its integrative unity. They would argue that the soul of a brain dead person is still present in the body but not operating through the brain. They see the position of brain death advocates as an attempt to separate the soul into parts: that is, the intellectual or thinking part of the soul leaves the body before the sensate and vegetative parts of the soul leave the body. They argue that if any function of the soul is still present, all parts are present since the soul is indivisible. They believe the vegetative powers of the soul are still intact since brain dead persons still breathe and process nutrition, and their organs have not begun to degenerate. The fact that the organs cannot operate without mechanical help does not mean that the powers of the soul are not present—rather, machines are assisting these powers.

Opponents of brain death criteria also note that different hospitals and different countries use different criteria to determine who qualifies as brain dead. That is, a person declared brain dead and suitable as an organ donor in one hospital may not be declared brain dead in another. Moreover, the time of death is not recorded as the moment when tests demonstrate that there is no integrated brain activity but rather when the organs are removed. Opponents of brain death argue that it is the removal of the organs that causes the death of the brain dead patient.

Some of those who do not accept brain death criteria for determining certain death nevertheless acknowledge that all further medical treatment of most of those who qualify as brain dead is extraordinary medical treatment and can be discontinued (a possible exception, for instance, would be a pregnant woman needing to be kept alive until her baby is born). They insist that the vital organs of brain dead persons, however, cannot morally be removed until they are declared dead by circulatory-respiratory criteria (failure to circulate oxygenated blood, rather than simply failure of the heart and lungs), for removing organs prior to that would in fact be causing the death of the donors.

These critics would argue that, while the shortage of

organs for transplant is regrettable, it is not moral to kill people to get their organs to help other people. Some advocate the "non-heart-beating" donor procedure, in which doctors harvest vital organs from a donor declared dead by circulatory-respiratory criteria (see question 46).

The Vatican has given cautious approval to determining death by neurological criteria. In the year 2000 Pope John Paul II addressed this matter in a talk given to the International Congress on Organ Transplants:

> With regard to the parameters used today for ascertaining death—whether the 'encephalic' [neurological] signs or the more traditional cardio-respiratory signs—the Church does not make technical decisions. She limits herself to the Gospel duty of comparing the data offered by medical science with the Christian understanding of the unity of the person, bringing out the similarities and the possible conflicts capable of endangering respect for human dignity.[10]

In other words, the Church leaves the theoretical medical question of what signs indicate death to technical experts in the field.

To the practical questions posed by people who are seeking or performing organ donation, the pope offered the following:

> Here it can be said that the criterion adopted in more recent times for ascertaining the fact of death, namely the *complete* and *irreversible* cessation of all brain activity, if rigorously applied, *does not seem to conflict* with the essential elements of a sound anthropology. Therefore a health-worker professionally responsible for ascertaining death can use these criteria in each individual case as the basis for arriving at that degree of assurance in ethical judgment which moral teaching describes

as *"moral certainty."* This moral certainty is considered the necessary and sufficient basis for an ethically correct course of action. Only where such certainty exists, and where informed consent has already been given by the donor or the donor's legitimate representatives, is it morally right to initiate the technical procedures required for the removal of organs for transplant.[11]

"Moral certainty" means having solid and reasonable evidence that a claim is true; it does not mean that we are completely certain or that further evidence might not change our decision. Even though theoretical questions might exist about the signs or determination of biological death, it is acceptable to use brain death criteria to determine death.

At present Catholics who believe that patients declared "brain dead" are truly dead may certainly act upon that belief, since the Vatican has approved brain death criteria for practical purposes. Nonetheless, at the time of this writing, the Vatican continues to study this question.

Question 46: What is the "non-heart-beating donor" procedure for obtaining organs? Is it morally acceptable?

The first heart used as an organ transplant was taken from a donor who was declared dead by traditional cardiopulmonary criteria. Generally those who have been declared dead by these criteria do not qualify as donors of vital organs, since organs quickly degenerate when oxygen is no longer perfusing them.

Recently doctors have perfected a new method of obtaining organs for transplant that does not involve brain death criteria. This method involves a non-heart-beating donor. The advantage of this protocol is that it avoids the controversies of brain death criteria noted in the previous question.

The donor in this procedure is a patient for whom any further treatment is extraordinary. The patient is taken to the operating room, and life support systems are discontinued there. After a physician determines the patient to be dead by traditional cardiopulmonary criteria, another team of physicians begins an operation to procure organs.

The Church does not have an official position on this procedure. Some Catholics consider it to be in accord with Catholic moral principles if very carefully delineated protocols are followed. For instance, they require that only severely brain-injured patients are eligible and that very conservative criteria for death be used.[12]

Others consider the procedure to be a violation of Catholic moral principles, largely because it puts dying or severely compromised patients at risk of being exploited for their organs. The primary concern with the protocols is the number of abuses to which they are susceptible.[13]

Some protocols require the administration of drugs to help preserve the organs for transplantation, and these drugs can hasten the death of the donor as a side effect. Some protocols are not confined to those who are severely brain-injured. There have also been reports of individuals considered suitable to be non-heart-beating donors who resisted pressure to donate organs and eventually recovered many of their functions.

Certainly, to be moral, the protocols for these procedures must involve measures to ensure that the patient (or designated proxy) has agreed to the organ donation, that any further treatment would truly be extraordinary, that the patient (or proxy) has refused further treatment as extraordinary, that no pressure has been put upon the patient (or proxy) to permit this procedure and that the team of doctors determining the time of death is different from the team of doctors procuring the organs for transplantation. If the procedure leads to serious abuses of the dying, for prudential reasons it should be avoided. Nonetheless, ethicists should be eager to explore this procedure as well as any other procedures that may provide moral ways for procuring organs for transplantation.

Question 47: Do hospital futility policies accord with Catholic morality?

Medical treatment is truly futile when it does not achieve the end sought. For instance, if a patient is taking medication to control blood pressure but his blood pressure does not respond to the treatment, the medication is futile and should be stopped.

Common sense dictates that it is foolish—and immoral—to engage in action that has no benefit. It is immoral because it is a waste of valuable resources. If treatment is truly futile, it should definitely be stopped.

In recent years a new understanding of futility has emerged. In the futility policies of most hospitals today, *futility* is rarely defined clearly. It applies vaguely to any treatment a physician or hospital no longer wants to provide for a patient, since he or they believe the patient's life to be no longer worth preserving and the overall care of the patient to be too expensive. Since the treatment is not restoring the patient to a life that is considered worth sustaining, the treatment is called "futile." In such a case it is not the *treatment* that is deemed futile or worthless; rather the *life* of the patient is deemed no longer worthy of treatment.

Even though a patient may want a treatment and be able to afford it, and even though the treatment may be achieving precisely the end sought, the judgment of the physician that the treatment is futile may lead to its cessation. For instance, a futility policy was used to deny a ventilator and dialysis treatment to a patient who was brain damaged (her motor abilities were impaired) but whose mental capacity was unaffected. She was able to communicate her desire to keep living.[14]

Determining futility in terms of whether or not someone's life is worth living does not accord with Church teaching, which views every human life as worth living (see question 38). It is moral to stop extraordinary treatment, and truly futile treatment should be stopped, but ordinary treatment must always be provided, even if it does not restore patients to a level of existence that people consider "worth living."

Texas law regarding futility is setting the standard for such policies elsewhere, which is unfortunate. According to that policy, if there is a disagreement between a physician who judges a treatment to be futile and a patient who wants to continue treatment, the physician is permitted to ask the patient to transfer to another hospital that will provide the disputed care. The physician needs to get permission from the hospital bioethics board, and the patient or his or her proxy decision maker can present counterarguments to the board. If the bioethics board agrees with the physician, the hospital must help the patient locate another hospital to provide care. If within ten days a hospital is not found, the first hospital is authorized to discontinue care.

Futility policies that put life-and-death decisions into the hands of physicians and bioethics boards give patients and their families very little time, at a very stressful time, to find suitable health care. Just as lawyers are not permitted to drop a case until another lawyer is found, so too physicians and hospitals should not refuse to treat a desperately ill patient unless alternative care is available.

Question 48: What is the sacrament of the sick? When should Catholics have recourse to it?

The *Catechism of the Catholic Church* informs us that the anointing of the sick "is not a sacrament for those only who are at the point of death. Hence, as soon as anyone of the faithful begins to be in danger of death from sickness or old age, the fitting time for him to receive this sacrament has certainly already arrived [cf. SC 73; cf. CIC, cann. 1004 § 1; CCEO, can. 738]" (*CCC*, 1514). The *Catechism* tells us that "the faithful should encourage the sick to call for a priest to receive this sacrament" (*CCC*, 1516). Family and friends of Catholic patients should remind them of this sacrament and possibly help locate a priest to celebrate the sacrament for them.

The sacrament of the sick is intended to provide graces to those who are gravely ill. The *Catechism* states: "The first grace of this sacrament is one of strengthening, peace and courage to overcome the difficulties that go with the condition of serious illness or the frailty of old age" (*CCC*, 1520). The sacrament also helps the sick unite their sufferings to those of Christ, and as an act of the Church, it enables the

Church to extend Christ's saving presence in this world. Finally, the sacrament prepares the dying for the final journey into life everlasting.

Only a priest can perform this sacrament, and the sacraments of penance and the Eucharist often accompany it. When those who are dying receive the Eucharist, it is called the *viaticum*—a Latin word that means "with you, on the way." Jesus greets us in this life through baptism, and he accompanies us as we "pass over" to our particular judgment and (we hope) our heavenly Father.

Only those who are seriously ill or about to undergo a serious operation may receive the anointing of the sick, but all Catholics, especially those undergoing the trials of less serious illnesses, should regularly receive the other sacraments. Catholic hospitals provide pastoral services that include visits by eucharistic ministers to bring the Eucharist to those who are ill. Many non-Catholic hospitals also have services that facilitate contact with priests or pastoral ministers. These will visit the sick, pray with them and bring the Eucharist. Catholics who are very ill, their family and their friends should pray and ask others to pray for them.

Sickness, especially serious illness, can be a time of profound spiritual growth. Many great saints, perhaps most famously Saint Francis of Assisi and Saint Ignatius Loyola, began their commitment to holiness as a result of illness. A health crisis can be a turning point for good when it reminds the sick person and others of the most important things in life and banishes illusionary trivialities. The sacrament of the sick, a continuation of Jesus' own ministry to the ill, powerfully aids those suffering from serious illness and provides an opportunity to encounter Christ's healing power.

CHAPTER SIX

Cooperation With Evil

Question 49: Sometimes health care professionals are asked to perform actions that may make them guilty of cooperating with the evil actions of others, such as assisting in abortion. How do these workers know when they must refuse to do certain things?

Virtually everyone cooperates with evil to some extent and with some regularity. That is, things we do make it possible for others to engage in immoral behavior. We purchase items made by companies that treat their employees unfairly, and we pay taxes to governments that have immoral polices and practices—for instance, paying for abortions. We are not held morally accountable for all such cooperation, although when we are in a position to change or protest such practices, we should do so.

The type of cooperation with moral evil that is most serious is when we fully intend that the evil with which we are cooperating should be done. For example, the boyfriend who wants his girlfriend to get an abortion, drives her to the abortion clinic and gives her money to pay for the abortion shares fully in the guilt of the abortion. Similarly, when an accomplice drives the getaway car for a bank robbery, he shares in the sin of theft, even though he does not open the safe.

Such cooperation is called "formal cooperation" with evil. (The word *formal* is derived from the philosophic term *form*, which pertains to the essence of something.) *Formal cooperation* means that the cooperator fully aligns his or her will with that of the primary agent. The formal cooperator truly chooses that the act be done.

Yet sometimes even those who do not want an action to happen are still guilty of a kind of cooperation with evil that is morally equivalent to formal cooperation with evil. Consider a boyfriend who does not want his girlfriend to get an abortion. Perhaps he even tries to convince her not to get the abortion. Nonetheless, he drives the girlfriend to the clinic and pays for the abortion. Because he does not will or choose that she get an abortion, he is not guilty of formal cooperation with evil. Yet his material support makes him inextricably and immediately tied up in her act of getting an abortion.

The boyfriend is guilty of what is known as "immediate material cooperation in evil." The word *immediate* here means that the cooperation is directed precisely to the evil being committed. Morally such cooperation is equivalent to formal cooperation with evil. The boyfriend has sinned seriously.

Similarly, someone who tries to talk a friend out of robbing a bank but drives the friend to the bank so that he might rob it is guilty of immediate material cooperation with evil. In spite of the fact that the driver does not want the robbery to happen, his voluntary cooperation is so direct and essential to the performance of the action that he is guilty of the deed performed. Nurses who oppose abortion but who help doctors perform them are in a situation of immediate material cooperation with evil.

Another form of material cooperation is not so direct and immediate. "Mediate" material cooperation refers to nonessential and indirect assistance that one provides to the performance of an immoral action. For instance, a firm that cleans a building in which an abortion clinic is housed is not contributing directly to the performance of abortions but is nevertheless aiding it.

Generally, if there is no necessity that one participate in mediate material cooperation with evil, one should not do so. The cleaning firm in the example should attempt to talk the landlord out of renting to the abortion clinic. If unsuccessful in getting the abortion clinic evicted and if not financially dependent upon the income from the cleaning contract, the firm should drop the account. When it is for some reason necessary that one cooperate with evil in a mediate material way, one should take actions, if possible, that to some extent counteract that cooperation.

Cooperation with evil that is not essential to the action and far removed from the action is called remote material cooperation. In these instances the contribution to the evil is insignificant; the deeds would be done without the cooperation. The person provides something that assists the primary agent in performing the task, but he or she does not align his or her will with that of the evildoer: that is, it cannot reasonably be said that the person chose that the evil actions happen.

Remote material cooperation with evil involves no guilt unless, of course, one easily can avoid that cooperation. For example, if it is easy to buy tennis shoes from a manufacturer that does not use third-world child labor, one should certainly do so, but one is not always obliged to research the policies of various manufacturers or suppliers.

We will use these categories of cooperation with evil to answer further questions of morality that health care providers face.

Question 50: Is it moral for a Catholic pharmacist to fill prescriptions for contraceptives? Is it moral for a Catholic nurse to give Depo-Provera shots?

As the discussion of question 25 explained, the Catholic Church teaches that contraception violates God's plan for sexuality and is intrinsically evil. Contraception itself is a serious sin, compounded when the mechanism by which the contraceptive works is an abortifacient one: that is, when the contraceptive works by preventing the implantation of an embryonic human being in his or her mother's uterus. The question of the morality of filling prescriptions for contraceptives requires that we employ some terms we just explained, formal and material cooperation in evil.

A factor that complicates this analysis is that some contraceptives can be used for moral purposes, even though it is never moral to contracept. Question 27 explains the morality of the therapeutic use of the contraceptive pill. In that instance a woman is not using the pill *as a contraceptive—that is, her intention is not to make herself infertile*—but is using the hormones that are in the pill *to treat a medical pathology* such as endometriosis. It is true that most women using hormone treatments that cause infertility are doing so precisely so they can be infertile. Yet a pharmacist has no routine way of knowing which women are using the pill for contraceptive purposes and which are using it for therapeutic purposes.

Consider the plight of a gun salesman who sells guns to policemen and soldiers and security guards. This work is perfectly moral. Yet suppose he has a particular gun in stock that is sometimes used for moral purposes but mostly for immoral activities, sometimes even to kill innocent people. If the salesman has any way of knowing the intention of the individual purchasing the gun, he should refuse to sell it to those who will be using it for immoral purposes, even at the risk of losing his job. Otherwise his cooperation with evil is simply too immediate.

Pharmacists are in a similar situation. That is, some women who use the contraceptive pill may be using it to treat physical conditions for which the hormones in the pill are helpful. It is moral for a pharmacist to fill those prescriptions. But most of the women picking up contraceptives from a pharmacy are using them for contraceptive purposes, an intrinsically wrong action. Moreover, since the chemical contraceptives occasionally work by preventing a new little human being from implanting in his or her mother's uterus, the use of these contraceptives is even more gravely immoral.

So should a pharmacist fill a prescription for the pill? Some moralists think that pharmacists have a moral obligation to refuse to fill prescriptions for RU 486, which is not a contraceptive but a pill that works exclusively by causing an early abortion. On the other hand, they argue that filling prescriptions for other chemical contraceptives is remote cooperation with evil and morally permissible for the following reasons: (1) filling such prescriptions is only a small part of what the pharmacist does; (2) the pharmacist does not know whether the contraceptives are being prescribed for therapeutic purposes; and (3) the contraceptives have an abortifacient effect only occasionally. They also argue that it would not be immoral to sell condoms, since they harm only the individual using them.

Others argue that, unless alerted otherwise, it is reasonable for a pharmacist to assume that contraceptives are going to be used for immoral purposes and that over a period of time the abortifacient effect is highly likely. They also argue that the condom used as designed has no moral purpose. Further, the connection between the use of contraceptives and increased incidence of unwed pregnancy, abortion, divorce and poverty is so well established that the harm done is not confined to the individuals involved. They believe that a pharmacist should refuse to fill prescriptions for contraceptives unless he or she is confident that they are being prescribed for therapeutic purposes.

A similar conflict faces a nurse who is asked to give a patient a Depo-Provera shot and who knows that the shot is being given for contraceptive purposes. This seems somewhat different from filling a prescription for the pill, since a woman may or may not decide to take the pills: one more act of the will—that is, the free choice of the woman—stands between the material supplying of the pill and the immoral action of contraception. So the pharmacist has some distance from the act that the nurse does not have. When he or she gives the shot in accordance with the will of the patient, the intent to contracept has been set, and thus his or her cooperation with the immoral deed is more direct or immediate. Most Catholic ethicists would judge it immoral for nurses to give a Depo-Provera shot for a woman they know to be using it for contraceptive purposes.

The Church has no articulated teaching on these matters. Although experts disagree on the proper application of principle, some guidance can be taken from the fact that the USCCB have asked that legislators pass laws to protect pharmacists who have a conscientious objection to filling prescriptions for contraceptives.

Question 51: What is scandal? In the practice of medicine, what kind of behavior causes scandal?

The *Catechism of the Catholic Church* states, "Scandal is an attitude or behavior which leads another to do evil. The person who gives scandal becomes his neighbor's tempter. He damages virtue and integrity; he may even draw his brother into spiritual death. Scandal is a grave offense if by deed or omission another is deliberately led into a grave offense" (*CCC*, 2284). The *Catechism* continues: "Scandal takes on a particular gravity by reason of the authority of those who cause it or the weakness of those who are scandalized" (*CCC*, 2285).

Scandal occurs when an individual who has influence over others says or does something that might lead others into sin. This involves supporting activity that is wrong either explicitly or implicitly.

Health care professionals rightly enjoy considerable prestige and a high level of respect and trust among those they serve. Physicians and nurses are considered to be compassionate and responsible individuals who will help others, not harm them. Thus they need to take particular care that their words and their behavior do not lead others astray.

For instance, Catholic hospitals should do their best not to hire physicians who engage in practices that are opposed to Church teaching, such as prescribing contraceptives for contraceptive purposes. Catholic physicians should try to avoid partnerships with those who engage in practices against Church teaching. Individual Catholics should attempt to engage as their physicians only those who practice medicine in accord with Catholic moral principles.

Sometimes finding physicians who conduct their practices fully in compliance with Catholic moral principles is difficult, if not impossible, in our culture. Given the contemporary reality, the principle of duress or necessity would permit a Catholic hospital to hire a physician who does not abide by Church teaching, a Catholic physician to join a practice with physicians who do not abide by Church teaching or a Catholic patient to have a physician who does not abide by Church teaching. A hospital that out of necessity hires a physician who engages in immoral practices should try all the harder to hire physicians who abide by Church teaching.

In some communities a Catholic hospital and a secular hospital have merged out of economic necessity. Often intense conflict arises over the community's desire for the continuation of immoral practices such as abortion, provision of contraceptives and sterilization on the one hand and the refusal of a Catholic hospital to cooperate with such practices on the other. Sometimes compromises are forged that distance the Catholic hospital from such practices and protect the Catholic hospital from immoral cooperation with evil and scandal. Catholic hospitals nonetheless sometimes find themselves in closer connection with evil than they would like, since in spite of care taken, some of the public will believe that the Catholic hospital is involved in immoral cooperation with evil, while others will believe the hospital to be indifferent to the health care needs of some of the populace.

In these situations it may be helpful for local church leaders to wage an aggressive educational campaign. Church leaders should explain the reasons for entering the merger, why the Church views the controversial practices as immoral and why the compromises made are moral ones.

Physicians who belong to groups whose members engage in immoral practices should attempt to convince their colleagues to abandon those practices and, if prudent to do so, should distance themselves publicly from the immoral practices of the group. Sometimes these relationships can provide opportunities for Catholic physicians and patients to give witness to their faith. But if Catholic physicians are benefiting directly from the ill-gotten gains of their partners, or if they cannot avoid giving scandal, they should seek all the more energetically practices that are compatible with their moral commitments.

Sometimes a high price must be paid for being true to one's faith. Hospitals may be unable at times to provide services to valued patients; physicians may have to be content with a lower income; and patients may have to decline the services of otherwise very competent physicians.

Question 52: Is it moral to use vaccines that have been produced from aborted fetuses?

A number of vaccines for common diseases, such as rubella or German measles, were made through use of cell lines generated from aborted fetuses. Some parents refuse to allow their children to get these vaccines, since they believe that to do so would amount to cooperation with the evil of abortion.

The Vatican has produced a very nuanced judgment on this question.[1] It strongly condemns the use of aborted fetuses for such purposes and judges those who produced the vaccine to be guilty of formal cooperation with the evil of abortion—that is, they share the guilt of those who performed the abortions. It judges as guilty of material cooperation with evil (see question 49) those who continue to produce the vaccine, distribute it and do not condemn the origin of the vaccine or work to find a new source for it. They too are doing something immoral.

In spite of the serious moral culpability of those who initially produced the vaccine and some of those who continue to produce and distribute it, the Vatican does not hold physicians and parents who elect to vaccinate children morally culpable if (1) no alternatives are available; (2) they work to encourage researchers to find new, morally unproblematic sources for the vaccines; (3) there are serious health risks in refusing the vaccine; and (4) this is viewed as a temporary solution. These physicians and parents are involved in a "very remote material cooperation" with the evil of abortion and "an immediate passive material cooperation with regard to their marketing."[2] Such forms of cooperation are permissible under some circumstances. The serious health risks of such diseases as rubella present such circumstances.

Some Catholics find it difficult to accept the Vatican's judgment that limited use of vaccines from aborted fetuses is morally permissible. Since abortion is intrinsically evil, they think there should be no cooperation with it, no matter how remote, material or necessary. Some liken the use of vaccines from aborted fetuses to the use of medical knowledge gained by the Nazis in their severe mistreatment of Jews. Since this knowledge dishonors the memory of the Jews experimented on by the Nazis, they consider it immoral to use the knowledge gained.

Some believe that it is intrinsically wrong to take advantage of ill-gotten gains, and since vaccines produced through use of fetal tissues from aborted human beings are ill-gotten gains, no one should ever make use of such vaccines. Yet this principle is not one advanced by the Church. For example, the Church will permit the use of organs from individuals who have been murdered. The Church, however, would not allow organ transplants if individuals were being murdered in order to get the organs. It is then permissible in some circumstances to take ill-gotten gains and use them for the good; in other circumstances it is not.

The question of the use of vaccines from aborted fetuses falls into some murky middle ground. The abortions that yielded the tissues from which vaccines were made were done long ago, and no more babies are being aborted to keep the vaccine going. Those who wish to use the vaccine to help their children are not supporting the abortion industry in any direct or significant way. Yet there is still a "taint" of abortion that hangs over the vaccines, such that to use them risks scandal—that is, those using them risk leading others to believe that one does not fully value fetal life. In a culture of death, some people believe, all those who value life must attempt to distance themselves from anything that may serve to perpetuate that culture.

The Vatican is concerned that continued use of the vaccines without condemnation of their origins and without attempts to find new moral sources threatens to make abortion a more acceptable procedure. Thus the guiding principle could be formulated: We should not use ill-gotten gains if in doing so we perpetuate the evil—that is, unless our use of the ill-gotten gain is sufficiently remote from the evil and the need for the gain is sufficiently serious.

The Vatican notes that in a culture where abortion is legal and widely practiced, everyone must be willing to sacrifice a great deal to avoid any behavior that may perpetuate the practice of abortion. It is of great importance that pressure be put on governments and pharmaceutical companies to find moral sources for vaccines. Some parents may feel called to participate in a kind of "conscientious objection" to the use of tainted vaccines and refuse them, even though their children may be exposed to serious health risks. In the final analysis, however, it is moral to use such vaccines in order to protect one's children if no alternative is available.

Question 53: Is it morally acceptable to separate conjoined twins?

Conjoined twins are sometimes called Siamese twins, after a famous case of conjoined twin brothers from Siam, now Thailand, who toured as part of P.T. Barnum's Circus in the nineteenth century. Conjoined twins result when a single human embryo begins to split but fails to entirely divide into two identical twins. They occur only in about one of two hundred thousand births, and almost half of all conjoined twins are stillborn. For those who survive the question arises, is it morally permissible to separate them?

Since conjoined twins can be joined in a variety of ways, there is no one answer that applies to all cases. Separating those who are joined in a rather superficial way involves no serious danger to either twin. In such cases, so long as both twins consent or the parents consent in cases of minor children, there is no ethical problem in separating what is unnaturally joined.

Sometimes the separation of the twins cannot take place without grave risk. In the worst-case scenario, the well-being of one twin depends upon the other in such a way that separating them will result in the death of one twin. These twins are known as "asymmetric conjoined twins."

Treatment for asymmetric conjoined twins may vary depending on the details of the situation, but the case of English twins "Jodie" and "Mary" helps illustrate the principles involved. This case was particularly difficult, since without separation both twins would die, but surgery to separate them would result in the immediate death of the weaker twin, Mary. She shared Jodie's aorta, and the strain of pumping blood for two bodies would eventually result in Jodie's death as well as Mary's. Jodie was expected to survive surgery, but Mary would not because her heart could not continue to beat without the benefit of Jodie's aorta.

Some ethicists objected to the separation of Jodie and Mary as a case of intentional killing. Mary would be killed, they believed, in order to save Jodie. But as we saw in the question on double effect (question 9), the inevitability of an effect or consequences does not lead to the conclusion that the effect was intended.

Indeed, although Mary's death was a foreseen effect of the separation, nothing in the procedure was directed toward killing Mary.[3] The surgeons restored to Jodie the aorta that belonged to her, and in the process Mary died. Restoring vital organs to their rightful owner is a moral thing to do. In other words, the separation itself was not killing.

Double effect reasoning clarifies why the separation was justified:

1. Neither restoring organs to their rightful owners nor separating conjoined twins is in itself evil.

2. The evil effect of Mary's death was not intended.

3. The evil effect of Mary's death was not a means to the good of saving Jodie's life.

4. Saving Jodie's life was a proportionately serious reason for allowing the evil effect of Mary's death.

A final question was involved in the case of Jodie and Mary. Against the wishes of the parents of the girls, judges ordered that the separation take place. Was the separation of Mary and Jodie morally obligatory? Was the judge right to override the wishes of the parents?

Here we believe the answer is no. Generally there is no obligation to separate conjoined twins although it is certainly natural and right to want to do so. As noted in question 40, extraordinary means include treatments with significant burdens for others, treatments with low chances of success, costly treatments, treatments that are psychologically repugnant and treatments that are experimental.

One assesses the burdens and benefits of *treatments*, not the burdens and benefits of *human lives*.

Although not excessively risky for Jodie, separating Jodie and Mary was significantly burdensome in terms of financial cost, psychological repugnance for both parents and its experimental nature. Obviously, the burden to Mary was tremendous, for it cost Mary her life. So although this separation procedure was morally permissible, the parents were not morally obliged to choose it for their children.

In principle the separation of conjoined twins does not constitute killing, even if a side effect is that one of the twins may or will certainly die. Yet such surgeries should not be made obligatory but rather should be a permissible option, to be chosen with due deliberation and care for the well-being of all involved.

Question 54: Is it moral to have a healthy breast removed because of a genetic propensity to breast cancer?

Breast cancer is the most common form of cancer among women and the second leading cause of death for women. Genetic testing can reveal that some women are at a very high risk of getting breast cancer. Various preventative measures are available to them, involving either chemotherapy or surgery. Such measures have a very high rate of success.

The Church's condemnation of mutilation concerns such practices as the sexual mutilations common in some cultures and, for instance, amputations of healthy limbs simply because people want to belong to amputee groups. What is immoral about these practices is that they prevent the body from performing its natural functions as a means to achieving extraneous ends. Surgery to remove a portion of the body that has a high probability of developing in such a way as to threaten the person's life does not constitute mutilation.

Indeed, it is common medical practice to remove wisdom teeth that are not currently causing any problems. Sometimes a portion of a colon exhibiting a precancerous condition is removed. These conditions in themselves are not unhealthy, but they predispose someone to future illness.

The removal of a healthy breast from a woman who has a high probability of developing cancer is analogous. (Determining at what age such a procedure is warranted may be somewhat difficult, but actuarial tables can tell when some women are likely to develop cancer.) Certainly, treatments and procedures that do not involve removal of a breast and that have a comparable success rate should be used first. Nonetheless, since the parts of the body serve the whole and since a breast easily attacked by cancer threatens the whole, at least incipiently, it would be moral for a woman to have one or both breasts removed to prevent the onset of cancer.

Question 55: What if a patient cannot be persuaded to do what is morally correct?

As question 4 stated, everyone should follow his or her conscience, after doing one's best to correctly form the conscience. But sometimes consciences can be wrong.

Respect for persons requires respect for their conscientious decisions. Thus others must respect wrong decisions of conscience if doing so does not involve immoral cooperation with evil (see question 49). Physicians must respect the decisions of their patients unless doing so would violate their consciences, for physicians also deserve respect.

Disagreements between patients and physicians on what is obligatory treatment can be very difficult to resolve.

It is difficult to give guidance about such disputes, since the guiding principles can be so general as to be unhelpful. One general guideline that governs disputed treatment is that first and foremost patients have the right to make decisions about their medical treatment. In instances where the physician or family members believe that the patient is making a terrible mistake, one that could have dire consequences and perhaps even be fatal, they should try to persuade the patient to accept the appropriate treatment. Some legitimate and often effective ways of persuading a reluctant patient include carefully listening to the patient's concerns and trying to allay them, inviting a family member or a persuasive member of the hospital staff to converse with the patient and putting the patient in contact with someone who has had the procedure.

The physician should look for signs of depression that may be treatable; perhaps medicine or therapy can restore the patient to a sound decision-making capacity. The physician should also consider whether the patient has become incompetent to make a decision, perhaps because of psychological problems, dementia or simply being overwhelmed by the debilitation of the disease. When appropriate, the physician should call for a psychiatric consultation.

If a patient has designated a decision-making proxy, the proxy may be enlisted to help make difficult decisions. In rare cases our legal system will issue court orders to force a patient to receive treatment.

Moreover, as is always true with ethical decisions, a change in some aspect of the situation might change radically the moral decision. In some situations there are factors that are extremely difficult to articulate. For instance, sometimes the physician or family member believes that the patient will be truly grateful once the treatment begins working. The patient may have some personal reasons for rejecting the treatment, r0easons that will be forgotten once his or her condition improves. On the other hand, sometimes the physician or family member believes that a patient will be terribly hurt, become distrustful and withdraw if any attempt to force treatment is pursued. A patient's delicate relationship with God might lie in the balance.

With the due caution that some alteration in facts might radically change the moral way to proceed, we are going to consider some specific cases (real ones) to demonstrate how the above principles might apply.

First let us consider a Catholic patient who refuses treatment that a Catholic physician believes is morally obligatory and in which the proper medical and moral choice is obvious. Suppose a pregnant woman with an infected uterus erroneously believes that she has an allergy to all chemicals. Her infection threatens to flare up and could be life threatening, both for herself and her unborn child. An antibiotic would treat the infection reliably, but the woman refuses to take antibiotics, falsely believing herself to be allergic to them.

The physician should do everything possible to persuade the patient to take the antibiotic. The physician should reason with her and call in the services of those who are particularly trusted by her or who are very persuasive. While an adult patient may have a legal right to refuse all treatment, this case is complicated by the dependence of the unborn child on the decisions of his or her mother. For this reason the physician may seek a court order to require the woman to take the antibiotic.

Other instances are not so clear. A patient may have reasons for refusing treatment that the physician finds unreasonable but must still respect. A physician in this position should evaluate the situation carefully to determine whether or not the patient has moral reasons for refusing treatment. The Church permits latitude in assessing whether a treatment is obligatory.

As with most expenditures and sufferings, there may be a considerable range of diversity in what is considered reasonable to spend or to endure for a possible benefit. Consider a sixty-five-year-old man diagnosed with cancer who has a year to live if he undergoes treatment and only three months if he refuses treatment. Whereas the physician may believe that gaining nine months would be worth the expenditure and suffering, the patient morally may refuse the treatment. The physician should respect the decision of the patient, once the physician has made very clear his reasoning concerning the issue.

The Church teaches that a patient may refuse treatment for which he or she has a psychological repugnance (see question 40). This category can be very difficult to determine. For instance, consider a woman who has a severe eating disorder and is suffering from intense psychological trauma from memories of sexual abuse. This individual has received psychotherapy for years and has experienced negligible improvement. She is on medication for depression and a variety of other ailments. The side effects of the medication give her horrible diarrhea.

The woman wishes to stop taking any treatment for the diarrhea (say, Imodium in pill form, which is inexpensive and has no side effects), knowing that she is likely to die from dehydration or heart failure, which is a likely cause of death even in her current situation. She wishes to die but would not take any direct action to cause her death.

The treatment for diarrhea is ordinary treatment and thus obligatory. So should the physician work to have the young woman committed and force the treatment for diarrhea? If she were hospitalized for another condition but refused food and water, should he get a court order to have her force-fed?

Objectively the woman appears to be seeking to commit suicide by omission, but her strong subjective repugnance to taking any more medicine into her body likely makes it wrong to consider her guilty of this. The physician, after trying valiantly to help her gain a will to live, may decide not to take any legal action to get her to comply. The patient perceives that forceful intrusions have ruined her life. What she needs now is loving care that respects her bodily integrity and her (admittedly unwise) decisions.

Question 56: Does a physician need to respect the decision of a Jehovah's Witness to refuse a blood transfusion?

This is a case similar to the previous one about the uncooperative patient, but here the reasons for rejecting treatment are not some peculiarity of the patient but a deeply held religious belief. Again, in general, physicians should respect the decisions of their patients, and they should especially respect decisions based on a religiously formed conscience. Only when decisions would lead to a life-threatening situation should physicians consider taking measures to force a patient to receive treatment and then only with great care.

For some period of time in the United States, it was routine for hospitals to get court orders to allow them to give blood transfusions both to minor children of Jehovah's Witnesses and to adult Jehovah's Witnesses. The views of both society and most Catholic theologians, however, have changed.

In society the emergence of autonomy as the foremost value in bioethics and the growing prevalence of relativism have produced a reluctance to override the decisions of private individuals in respect to what they do with their bodies. There has been some shift among Catholic ethicists due to a clarification of the requirements of the right to religious liberty, which of course is very different from relativism. The consensus in society and among Catholic theologians is that adult Jehovah's Witnesses should not be forced to receive blood transfusions. Reasonable efforts should be made to convince them to receive blood transfusions in cases of necessity, but their decisions should not be overridden.

Cases involving young children are treated differently. If a young child of a Jehovah's Witness, one who is not mature enough to make a decision on treatment, should need a blood transfusion in the face of death, it would be moral for a hospital, with the help of a court order, to give the transfusion. Civil laws generally are designed to give such court orders, since the state has responsibility for the common good, which includes protecting the lives of the innocent.

Though most Catholic theologians maintain that it would be moral for a physician to honor the adult Jehovah's Witness's religiously formed conscience, a physician morally could refuse to do surgery if he is not authorized to give a transfusion he considers likely to be necessary. Otherwise the physician may face a situation where he or she would have to violate the standards of morally necessary treatment.

Moreover, if an emergency situation arose involving someone known to be a Jehovah's Witness who had no opportunity to discuss treatment and for whom there is no proxy decision maker, a physician morally could give the transfusion. The physician must act in accord with objective moral standards.

Note that we use the phrase "morally could" rather than claim that the physician "must" do something. We do so because we are somewhat tentative in our judgment on this matter. The limitations on religious liberty include the rights of others, public order and public morality, and sometimes it is difficult to ascertain the proper way of honoring these in particular situations. Certainly some actions are so objectively wrong that even a religious justification for doing them should not be honored. If someone were to threaten to poison himself or others, allegedly because of a command from God, public authorities should prevent that action.

But this analogy does not totally settle the issue, since there are important differences between drinking poisoned Kool Aid and a Jehovah's Witness's refusal of a blood transfusion. First, a Jehovah's Witness is not refusing treatment as a means of intentionally killing himself or others. Second, forcing a medical treatment on another person's body is different from interfering with intentionally lethal actions. Judging whether a forced intrusion on someone's body truly qualifies as battery or whether it should be considered a rescue (like an emergency tracheotomy) is difficult.

To be moral, forced intrusions must be necessary and objectively good. It is also highly desirable, though not necessary in all cases, that the medical treatment be something the individual can be expected to want. Blood transfusions can qualify as necessary and objectively good, but if a Jehovah's Witness expressly has rejected one, it is hard to argue that he or she can be expected to want the intrusion. Yet the refusal of the treatment is not sufficient reason to determine that the person should not be forced to get it. We force people with some regularity to do what they oppose, and some of those procedures, such as vaccines, are intrusive.

Nonetheless, there may be situations when it would be right for a physician to honor a Jehovah's Witness's refusal of a blood transfusion for himself or in respect to children, even if it meant death for the adult or the child. People are permitted to do very foolish things, even things that threaten their lives and the lives of their children. Society attempts in many ways to protect people from their own choices and to protect children from the bad choices of their parents; again, vaccines are a good example.

What is key in this situation is the factor of religious liberty. Even though we believe that overriding an unconscious Jehovah's Witness's previous refusal of a blood transfusion may be objectively morally permissible, Catholic physicians may decide that it is best to honor the choices of a Jehovah's Witness. Forgoing a morally good action for the sake of the common good—in this case, the respect of the religious beliefs of others—can sometimes be the right thing to do.[4]

Question 57: What steps should a Catholic working at a Catholic hospital take in the face of evidence that the hospital or those working there are engaging in practices recognized by the Church as incompatible with true human dignity?

Almost everyone recognizes the importance of honesty, and this applies to institutions as well as individuals. Hospitals that call themselves Catholic and that rely on the financial support of Catholics should live up to their name in what they say as well as in what they do. Failures to do so are both dishonest and contrary to fundamental norms of truth in advertising. Unfortunately, some Catholic hospitals allow procedures such as tubal ligations that are forbidden by the Church.

Clearly, an employee first should be very certain that he or she both understands Church teaching correctly and has clear evidence that violations of that teaching are taking place. In such cases the employee should obtain as much objective evidence as possible as well as the testimony of others who have observed the immoral actions.

After the whistle-blower has taken these essential steps, he or she should consider carefully what to do next. Great care must be taken, because often the whistle-blower will be subject to retaliation, perhaps even loss of job and future employment possibilities and damage to his or her reputation. Yet we are all called to witness to the truth. The eighth beatitude tells us, "Blessed are those who are persecuted for righteousness' sake, for theirs is the kingdom of heaven" (Matthew 5:10). Telling the truth to people who are profiting from wrongdoing is a fairly common cause of persecution. In reference to the contemporary world, the beatitude might read: "Blessed are the persecuted, for they shall risk their jobs, their lives and so on."

Certainly, here as elsewhere, the whistle-blower should pray for guidance about what concrete steps to take. If other professionals at the hospital are knowledgeable about the violations and prepared to take action, they should attempt to work together. If the offense is strictly that of an individual physician, someone the physician trusts and respects should approach him or her, if at all possible, and explain that what he or she is doing is not in accord with the teaching of the Catholic Church and that the behavior needs to stop.

If the whistle-blower(s) believes that such action would be counterproductive—that is, perhaps it would enable the offender to hide evidence—the best process may be to talk to the offender's superior. Again, it is wise to find someone who knows how to approach the superior in a way that is likely to gain a respectful hearing. If there is good reason to believe that the superior would not take the right action, the whistle-blower may have to go even higher up the ladder of authority.

As with all such activity, the whistle-blower should keep careful documentation of all conversations and communications with the "accused." The whistle-blower may wish to avoid any private conversations with the person; having another witness to all exchanges can prevent having one's words and behavior misrepresented. If one wishes to write letters of complaint, it is very wise to have a prudent individual look over the letters to make certain that the language is clear and precise and the tone is civil and fair.

If the individual or the hospital refuses to make the changes necessary, it is proper to report the situation to the bishop of the diocese in which the hospital is located. The report should include full documentation of all evidence and communication. Again, having an individual whom the bishop trusts present the material would be best. Any correspondence should be marked "personal and confidential" and be sent by certified mail.

In fact, sometimes it is best to appeal directly to the bishop, especially if the offense is very serious. For instance, if physicians are performing abortions regularly (and there are known cases of physicians at Catholic hospitals doing abortions of defective unborn children), the bishop should be alerted immediately, especially if one has irrefutable evidence.

Finally, if neither the hospital nor the bishop takes appropriate action after a reasonable amount of time, it would be proper to report the offense to Rome. Guidance for doing so can be obtained from such organizations as the National Catholic Bioethics Center, www.ncbcenter.org.

Chapter Seven

The Ten Commandments for Health Care Professionals and Patients

The source of fundamental principles to guide Catholic bioethical judgments is, of course, the Ten Commandments, which make concrete the ultimate law of the moral life, love of God and love of neighbor. The familiarity of the Ten Commandments may make it difficult for us to see their applicability to the daily challenges of medical care. Here we are going to apply them both to some challenges that health care professionals frequently face and to behaviors that patients sometimes exhibit. The discussion in this section is more properly about ethics for health care professionals and those whom they serve than about bioethical issues.

I am the LORD your God.... You shall have no other gods before me (Exodus 19:2–3).

Although we have never seen doctors burning incense before golden calves or nurses bowing down before graven images, some false gods can tempt those in the medical profession. Sometimes physicians believe that life and death are ultimately in their control rather than the control of God, leading them to pursue a cure beyond what is reasonable and to subject a patient to undue suffering and expense. Other times they can judge that the burdens of life—say, for a severely challenged newborn—are too great to bear, and they recommend premature cessation of treatment or abortion because of fetal genetic defects. A third temptation is one that lures many of us, not just health care professionals: the desire for wealth.

Most of those who enter the health care professions are motivated by a desire to alleviate suffering, and that is, of course, a truly laudable motivation. Yet sometimes these professionals make the mistake of thinking that there is no higher good than that of ending suffering and keeping human beings alive. While watching one's patients suffer and die can be excruciating, there are times when health care professionals must honor the wishes of patients to forgo treatment that they judge to be unnecessary. One can see the rejection of the "I must do everything possible to prolong life" attitude in the Catholic teaching that extraordinary means need not be used to support human life (see question 40).

Another violation of this commandment is quite the opposite: namely, not preserving life when that should be done. This is another form of disrespect for God and perhaps the more common one. It is a failure to see the image and likeness of God in each human life. This may lead some health care providers to treat those with serious illness or disabilities as less than fully human and less deserving of respect.

Those who are less physically and mentally gifted are created by God and loved by God, no less than the greatest genius or most talented athlete. In fact, the disabled may deserve greater care. It is a privilege to care for them, since in their sufferings they live close to the cross of Christ.

The other false god—the desire to make a lot of money —can be the reason medical professionals pursue the careers they do. They then measure their success in life by how much money they make. Certainly money is necessary for many good things in this world, such as supporting a family and educating children. But physicians need to be very careful not to be unduly influenced by the fees that they will receive from the services they provide. They need to let integrity govern their decisions—for instance, about what tests to order, what treatments to prescribe and where to send patients for tests and treatments.

And medical professionals, like all of us, must be generous in donating their time and money to those who are less fortunate. Their lifestyles should not be lavish but rather fitting for those whose first love is not money, prestige or luxury but God himself.

Patients also can have false gods. They can make a god of their own health and comfort or the health and comfort of their loved ones. They can be excessively demanding of doctors and health care providers. They can insist on tests and treatments that their physicians consider unnecessary. Or they may value their own comfort so much that they are not willing to undergo treatments or lifestyle changes that would improve their well-being.

Patients too must make decisions in the light of the truths of the Catholic faith. For instance, they must decide which treatments to seek and which to refuse in the light of Church teaching and what they discern to be God's will for them.

You shall not take the name of the LORD your God in vain (Exodus 19:7).

This commandment enjoins respect for God's name and respect for the things and persons associated with God. Most directly this commandment requires that believers not swear: that in their speech they not utter vain expletives involving God's name. The work environment of hospitals—like all work environments—should be free of all forms of irreverent and foul speech.

This commandment expressed positively says that one must be reverent toward God's name. Prayer is a means of reverence. Though attending to the spiritual care of patients is not primarily the health care provider's job, offering to pray for and with one's patients is fitting for a Christian health care provider. Prayer consoles patients and has the real effect of supplying needed graces.

It is also appropriate that the whole ethos surrounding the care of patients should be Christian. Certainly the spiritual needs and beliefs of patients deserve respect, acknowledgment and, where appropriate, support. Catholic hospitals should provide spiritual care both to Catholics and other religious believers.

Patients should try to overcome the frustrations that come with diminishment of powers and the irritability that comes with fatigue and illness; they should not lapse into self-absorption or succumb to anger with God because of their suffering and the inconveniences they experience. They should take times of illness and debilitation as opportunities to rely upon the Lord. They should strive to make all their invocations of the Lord's name ones of praise, worship and humble petition.

Patients who exhibit a radical reliance on the Lord have been known to become God's means of converting unbelieving health care workers. For example, Francis Collins, the former chief of the Human Genome Project, reports in his book *The Language of God: A Scientist Presents Evidence for Belief* (New York: Free Press, 2006) that his own conversion to Christianity was sparked by encounters with believing patients.

Remember the Sabbath day, to keep it holy (Exodus 19:8).

Few people work longer hours than do health care professionals and those who support them. Their ability to endure long hard hours is admirable. But like a gas, professional work will expand to whatever space is allotted it. If the body and mind were not so weak, some people would work 24 hours a day, 365 days a year.

Those who take pride in their work and have a high standard of professional performance can succumb to finding their chief satisfaction in their accomplishments. Workaholic hours bring devastating consequences: divorce, breakdowns, inattentiveness on the job and depression, for instance. The humanity of health care professionals demands proper care of self, both body and soul.

People especially need to care for the self in relation to God. "The sabbath was made for man, not man for the sabbath" (Mark 2:17). Work is about what we do, but worship is about who we are: creatures made in the image of God. The Sabbath rest allows time to recreate and to recollect the fact that we work to live, not live to work. And we seek not merely to live but to have the fullness of life that comes from an intimate relationship with the True, Good and Beautiful. Catholic health care professionals should ensure that they get a day of rest each week and that they take time to pray and grow in their love of the Lord.

Common wisdom and studies have shown the health values of rest, of belief in God and of the practice of contemplation. One of the major contributions most people can make to their own good health is to lead a balanced life of work, recreation and worship. God, in fact, commands us to do so.

Patients also should honor the Sabbath. Though they may be confined to the hospital and unable to attend church, they can still offer God their prayer and their suffering. Indeed, for many people, the road to holiness began in earnest only in the hospital bed.

Honor your father and your mother (Exodus 19:12).

The work of health care professionals is so important that patients are rightly grateful for the services they receive. The long years of study and demanding apprenticeships, the long and hard hours and the high level of skill that health care professionals acquire make them worthy of profound respect. They will need to take care that their egos not become inflated. They must realize that, although their hard work is essential to their success, they are indebted to those who have provided them with education, training and an opportunity to practice.

Here "your father and your mother" can apply not just to one's biological parents but also to all those who have nurtured one through life and who continue to do so.

Medical professionals should see themselves not as superior individuals bestowing favors on the lowly but as beneficiaries of the many sacrifices of others. They should consider themselves privileged to hand on and contribute to the heritage that they have received.

The fourth commandment also enjoins the discharge of family duties not only toward parents and grandparents but also toward spouses and children. Parents who are doctors, nurses or other health care professionals should strive to be parents who deserve honor from their children, in part because of the quality and *quantity* of time they spend with them.

The honor that patients show their physicians is another manifestation of this commandment. Patients are right to show gratitude to those who serve and nurture them. They should realize that health care professionals, burdened by great demands, might not always live up to the high expectations others have of them. Patients should respect the needs of physicians for time away from the job and not solicit them for professional advice at social events, for instance.

You shall not kill (Exodus 19:13).

Although the Hippocratic Oath historically taken by physicians proscribes both abortion and euthanasia, these practices have become not only legal but also all too common. Given the prestige health care professionals enjoy in the community, they should give powerful personal witness to the value of human life. Catholic health care providers should refuse to cooperate in any way with procedures such as abortion, euthanasia and the starvation of severely disabled patients. They should also provide testimony when necessary to advance public opposition to these procedures.

Catholic health professionals should work to ensure that the practices in which they participate and the hospitals they serve fully honor the sanctity of human life. Catholic patients should give their full support to Catholic health care institutions and professionals who take a strong stand for the value of human life, and they should join in that witness.

You shall not commit adultery (Exodus 19:14).

In their personal lives, particularly because they are highly visible members of the community, health care professionals should try to model Christian virtues. Certainly they should be faithful to their marriage vows.

Taking advantage of a patient sexually is reprehensible. Such illicit relationships compromise the medical good of the patient and the service that a health care professional can provide by introducing elements that distract and complicate what is already by nature an intimate relationship. The characteristic disparity of power between doctor and patient, as well as the ordering of sexual acts to the context of marriage, require that adultery and fornication particularly be shunned in the context of medical treatment.

Moreover, when patients are suffering from the consequences of immoral sexuality, health care professionals must be alert to appropriate times for challenging patients to reform their lifestyles. Pointing out the health consequences of certain activities may deter some from continuing those activities. Helping patients recall or reevaluate their moral principles may also be a good health care measure. Physicians do not hesitate to discourage smoking and drinking; the health risks involved with many sexual practices are no less. Furthermore, sometimes health care professionals need to take courageous stands and refuse to prescribe medications or perform procedures that facilitate intrinsically evil acts, such as contraception and abortion.

Patients should be fully honest with their health care providers about their sexual histories, in order to ensure that they receive the proper treatment and that they do not put others at risk if they have untreated conditions.

You shall not steal (Exodus 19:15).

Health care professionals may not realize fully the various ways that they may be "stealing." Waste, duplication, fraud and abuse cost taxpayers, patients and insurance companies millions of dollars every year.

Health care professionals should keep on top of new developments in medicine and care; not to do so is to cheat one's patients. Patients should be able to expect that those who care for their health are giving them the best that the profession has to offer.

Patients should also be mindful of wasting the time and attention of health care professionals, whose resources are limited, and of demanding expensive tests that are unnecessary. They should take care of their health through diet and exercise so that they will have less need of expensive medical care.

You shall not bear false witness (Exodus 19:16).

Bearing witness to the truth is a foremost task of Christians. We should never willingly deceive those who deserve to know the truth. While there is some argument among theologians about whether it is immoral to say what is false to people intent on doing moral wrong with that truth, such as informing Nazis about the location of Jews, there is not disagreement about the fact that human relationships require trust and that lying to others undermines that trust. Physicians simply should not lie to their patients.

Although it is sometimes impossible to tell patients the whole truth about their conditions, truthfulness in what is said is possible. Most patients want to know the truth. Knowledge about even the most difficult truths liberates the patient from ignorance and allows him or her to decide (when necessary) how to meet death. Many people desire to put their affairs in order, financially and spiritually, before their final breath.

Telling difficult truths to patients requires what has been called a good "bedside manner." Physicians should be sensitive to the manner in which they convey difficult truths. They should choose their words carefully and involve family members when appropriate.

Given the astronomical awards resulting from many malpractice suits, physicians can be tempted to cover up their own mistakes and those of their colleagues. Yet transparency is necessary even when it is costly. Health care professionals must be honest about their own mistakes and be prepared to report the wrongdoings of others who may pose dangers to patients.

Patients too must be honest with health workers. For instance, they should not try to manipulate physicians into prescribing medications or doing tests by falsely reporting their symptoms. They must not file illegitimate lawsuits to gain unfair recompense.

You shall not covet your neighbor's wife...or anything that is your neighbor's (Exodus 19:17).

These commandments indicate that we are morally responsible not only for our actions but for our thoughts and desires as well. We should not desire what is not ours to possess, either sexually or materially.

Health care professionals must retain a respect for the human body in a context where it can easily be denigrated. They should not use their patients as fodder for sexual fantasy. They should be wary of disrespectful and crude discussions concerning sexual matters. Certainly physicians should not gossip about patients' sexual lives and should in every way respect the privacy of their patients.

Physicians should not get into competitive races for the nicest houses, cars or vacations or the greatest prestige.

Patients are right to want to be free of illness and suffering, but they should realize that coping with their situation is an opportunity to be particularly close to the suffering Christ. Illness and suffering are vocations of a kind. Patients should be grateful for whatever God sends them and not resent the good health and the benefits of good health that others enjoy.

The Ten Commandments are clear formulations of what we all should know is necessary for basic morality. Just as a soccer coach or a violin teacher will give injunctions to help a player or a musician achieve goals, so too God's commandments are not arbitrary hoops to jump through but rather means of attaining happiness on earth and perfect bliss in heaven. Health care professionals, like all conscious human beings, want this pure Life, pure Love and pure Light that we call God.

Helpful Resources

Catholic Bioethics in General

Church Documents

Pope John Paul II. *Evangelium Vitae,* Encyclical Letter on the Value and Inviolability of Human Life, March 25, 1995. www.vatican.va

Pope John Paul II. *Salvifici Doloris,* Apostolic Letter on the Christian Meaning of Human Suffering. February 11, 1984. www.vatican.va

Books

Cataldo, Peter J. and Albert S. Moraczewski, eds. *Catholic Health Care Ethics: A Manual for Ethics Committees.* Boston: National Catholic Bioethics Center, 2002.

Hayes, Edward J., Paul J. Hayes, Dorothy Ellen Kelly and James J. Drummey. *Catholicism and Ethics: A Medical/ Moral Handbook.* Norwood, Mass.: C.R. Publications, 1997.

May, William. *Catholic Bioethics and the Gift of Human Life.* Huntington, Ind.: Our Sunday Visitor, 2000.

Journals

Ethics and Medics. Boston: National Catholic Bioethics Center. Bimonthly analysis of bioethical issues. Subscribe online at www.ncbcenter.org.

Linacre Quarterly. Wynnewood, Pa.: Catholic Medical Association. Subscribe online at www.cathmed.org.

National Catholic Bioethics Quarterly. Boston: National
   Catholic Bioethics Center. Subscribe online at
   www.ncbcenter.org.

Organizations and Web Sites

Catholic Health Care East: www.che.org

Catholic Medical Association: www.cathmed.org

International Association of Catholic Bioethicists:
   www.iacbweb.org

International Federation of Catholic Medical Associations:
   http://frblin.club.fr

Life Issues: www.lifeissues.net

The Linacre Centre: www.linacre.org

National Catholic Bioethics Center: www.ncbcenter.org

Pontifical Academy for Life: www.vatican.va

Pontifical Council for Health Pastoral Care:
   www.healthpastoral.org

United States Conference of Catholic Bishops Pro-life
   Office: www.nccbuscc.org/prolife

Chapter One: Fundamentals

Budziszewski, J. *Written on the Heart: The Case for Natural
   Law.* Downers Grove, Ill.: InterVarsity Press, 1997.

Cataldo, Peter J. "The Principle of the Double-Effect."
   Ethics and Medics 20:3 (March 1995).
   www.ncbcenter.org.

Dodson, Christopher. "Prudential Judgment." June 2004.
   www.ndcatholic.org.

George, Robert P. *A Clash of Orthodoxies: Law, Religion, and Morality in Crisis*. Wilmington, Del.: Intercollegiate Studies Institute, 2002.

Pope John Paul II. *Veritatis Splendor* (The Splendor of Truth). August 1993. www.vatican.va

Kaczor, Christopher. *The Edge of Life: Human Dignity and Contemporary Bioethics*. London: Springer, 2005.

_____. *Proportionalism and the Natural Law Tradition*. Washington: Catholic University of America Press, 2002.

Lowery, Mark. "Infallibility in the Context of Three Contemporary Developments." *Faith and Reason* 23:3, 4 (1997–1998), pp. 225–253.

Morrow, Thomas. "Forming a Catholic Conscience." *Homiletic and Pastoral Review*. April 1996. www.catholic.net.

Ratzinger, Joseph. "Conscience and Truth." February 1991. www.ewtn.com.

Chapter Two: Beginning-of-Life Issues

Alcorn, Randy. *Pro-Life Answers to Pro-Choice Arguments*. Sisters, Oreg.: Multnomah, 1992.

Ashley, Benedict and Albert Moraczewski. "Cloning, Aquinas, and the Embryonic Person." *National Catholic Bioethics Quarterly*, vol. 1, no. 2 (summer 2001), pp. 189–201.

Beckwith, Francis. *Defending Life: A Moral and Legal Case Against Abortion Choice*. Cambridge: Cambridge University Press, 2007.

Condic, Maureen. "The Basics about Stem Cells." *First Things* 119 (May 2002), pp. 30–34.

―――. "Life: Defining the Beginning and the End." *First Things* 133 (May 2003), pp. 50–54.

Lee, Patrick. *Abortion and Unborn Human Life*. Washington: Catholic University of America Press, 1996.

Chapter Three: Reproductive Technologies

Congregation for the Doctrine of the Faith. *Donum Vitae, Instruction on Respect for Human Life in Its Origin and on the Dignity of Procreation: Replies to Certain Questions of the Day*. February 22, 1987. www.vatican.va.

O'Malley, Bishop Sean. "In Vitro Fertilization: Ethical Implications and Alternatives." November 9, 2001. www.catholicculture.org.

Vatican's Mission to the United Nations. "The Views of the Holy See on Cloning." February 2003. www.catholicculture.org.

Chapter Four: Contraception, Sterilization and Natural Family Planning

Books, Articles and Talks

Chaput, Archbishop Charles J. "A Pastoral Letter to the People of God of Northern Colorado on the Truth and Meaning of Married Love." July 22, 1998. www.lifeissues.net.

Doyle, Fletcher. *Natural Family Planning Blessed Our Marriage: 19 True Stories*. Cincinnati: Servant, 2006.

Galeone, Bishop Victor. "Marriage: A Communion of Life and Love." July 10, 1003. www.ccli.org.

Pope John Paul II. *Familiaris Consortio,* Apostolic Exhortation on the Role of the Family in the Modern World. November 22, 1981. www.vatican.va.

Kippley, John F. and Sheila K. *The Art of Natural Family Planning.* Cincinnati: Couple to Couple League International, 1998.

Long, John L. *Sterilization Reversal: A Generous Act of Love: Twenty Couples Share Their Stories.* Dayton: One More Soul, 2003.

Pope Paul VI. *Humanae Vitae.* Encyclical on the Regulation of Birth. July 25, 1968. www.vatican.va. The authors recommend the translation of *Humanae Vitae* by Janet E. Smith: online at www.aodonline.org

Smith, Janet E. "Contraception: Why Not?" New and revised CD and audiotape, www.mycatholicfaith.org.

––––––. *Humanae Vitae: A Generation Later.* Washington: Catholic University of America Press, 1991.

––––––, ed. *Why Humanae Vitae Was Right: A Reader.* San Francisco: Ignatius, 1993.

West, Christopher. *Good News About Sex and Marriage.* Cincinnati: Servant, 2004.

Organizations and Web Sites

Billings Ovulation Method: www.billings-centre.ab.ca

Couple to Couple League: www.ccli.org

Family of the Americas: www.familyplanning.net

Natural Family Site: www.bygpub.com

Chapter Five: End-of-Life Issues

Books and Articles

Congregation for the Doctrine of the Faith. *Declaration on Euthanasia.* May 5, 1980. www.vatican.va.

Pope John Paul II. Address to the Eighteenth International Congress of the Transplantation Society. August 29, 2000. www.vatican.va.

Keown, John. *Euthanasia, Ethics and Public Policy: An Argument Against Legalisation.* Cambridge: Cambridge University Press, 2002.

Muskin, Philip R. "The Request to Die: The Role for a Psychodynamic Perspective on Physician-Assisted Suicide." *Journal of the American Medical Association* 279 (1998), pp. 323–328.

Web Site

International Task Force on Euthanasia and Assisted Suicide: www.internationaltaskforce.org

Chapter Six: Cooperation With Evil

Cataldo, Peter J. and John M. Haas. "Institutional Cooperation: The ERDs. This Principle of Cooperation Can Guide Collaboration with Other-than-Catholic Partners." *Health Progress* 83:6 (November–December 2002). www.chausa.org.

Catholic Health Care East. Articles on whistleblowing. www.che.org.

Catholic Health East Ethics Department. "Religious Diversity: The Limits of Accommodation." *e-Cases in Ethics.* www.che.org.

Vander Heeren, A. "Scandal." *New Catholic Encyclopedia.*
www.newadvent.org.

Web Site

Pharmacists for Life International: www.pfli.org

Notes

Chapter One: Fundamentals

1. The pope here quotes the Congregation for the Doctrine of the Faith, Declaration on Euthanasia, *Iura et Bona*, May 5, 1980, sec. IV.

2. The pope quotes the Declaration on Euthanasia, sec. II.

3. John Paul II, Apostolic Letter on the Christian Meaning of Human Suffering, February 11, 1984, www.vatican.va.

4. Jean Paul Sartre, *Existentialism and Human Emotions* (New York: Citadel, 1985), p. 63.

5. Texas Conference of Catholic Bishops, "On Withdrawing Artificial Nutrition and Hydration," *Origins* 20 (1990), pp. 53–55.

6. Catholic Bishops of Pennsylvania, "Nutrition and Hydration: Moral Considerations," 1991, rev. ed., 1999, www.pacatholic.org.

7. NCCB Committee for Pro-life Activities, "Nutrition and Hydration: Moral and Pastoral Reflections," 1992, www.usccb.org.

8. Pope John Paul II, "Address to the Participants in the International Congress on Life-Sustaining Treatments and Vegetative State: Scientific Advances and Ethical Dilemmas," March 20, 2004, no. 4, www.vatican.va.

9. Thomas Aquinas, *Summa Theologiae* II, 2, question 64, art. 7, www.newadvent.org.

Chapter Two: Beginning-of-Life Issues

1. Randy Alcorn, "Scientists Attest to Life Beginning at Conception," www.epm.org.

2. Peter Singer, *Practical Ethics,* 2nd ed. (Cambridge: Cambridge University Press, 1999).

3. Mother Teresa's Letter to the U.S. Supreme Court on *Roe v. Wade,* February 1994, www.tldm.org

4. Maureen Condic, "Life: Defining the Beginning by the End," *First Things* 133 (May 2003), pp. 50–54, www.firstthings.com.

5. Lee M. Silver, *Remaking Eden: Cloning and Beyond in a Brave New World* (New York: Avon, 1997), p. 39.

6. Simon Barnes, "I'm Not a Saint, Just a Parent," *Times Online: The Best of The Times and The Sunday Times,* November 13, 2006, www.timesonline.co.uk

7. See Maureen L. Condic, "The Basics About Stem Cells," *First Things* 119 (January 2002), www.firstthings.com.

8. Condic, "The Basics About Stem Cells."

9. See the Center for Bioethics and Human Dignity joint statement "Production of Pluripotent Stem Cells," www.cbhd.org.

10. David L. Schindler, "*Veritatis Splendor* and the Foundations of Bioethics: Notes Towards an Assessment of Altered Nuclear Transfer and Embryonic (Pluripotent) Stem Cell Research," *Communio* 32 (Spring 2005), pp. 195–201.

11. Pietro Ramellini, "Some Critical Comments on Oocyte-Assisted Reprogramming," *The National Catholic Bioethics Quarterly* 5:4 (Winter 2005), pp. 658–660; Adrian J. Walker, "Altered Nuclear Transfer: A Philosophical Critique," *Communio* 31 (Winter 2004), pp. 649–684.

12. There are reports of successful transfers. See C.J. Wallace, "Transplantations of Ectopic Pregnancy from Fallopian Tube to Cavity of Uterus," *Surgery, Gynecology and Obstetrics*

24 (1917), pp. 578–579; Landrum B. Shettles, "Tubal Embryo Successfully Transferred in Utero," *American Journal of Obstetrics and Gynecology* 163 (1990), pp. 2026–2027.

13. See Wallace, Shettles.

14. For support of all of the above procedures see Albert S. Moraczewski, "Managing Tubal Pregnancies: Part I," *Ethics & Medics* 21:6 (June 1996), and "Managing Tubal Pregnancies: Part II," *Ethics & Medics* 21:8 (August 1996). For a critique of these articles, see William E. May, "Methotrexate and Ectopic Pregnancy," *Ethics & Medics* 23:3 (March 1998). See also Moraczewski's response, "Ectopic Pregnancy Revisited," *Ethics & Medics* 23:3 (March 1998). These articles are available online at www.ncbcenter.org (subscription needed). Also of interest is Christopher Kaczor's "Moral Absolutism and Ectopic Pregnancy," *Journal of Medicine and Philosophy* 26:1 (February 2001), pp. 61–74.

15. United States Conference of Catholic Bishops, "Moral Principles Concerning Infants With Anencephaly," September 19, 1996, www.nccbuscc.org.

Chapter Three: Reproductive Technologies

1. The Church document that covers reproductive technologies is by the Sacred Congregation for the Doctrine of the Faith, *Donum Vitae,* "Instruction on Respect for Human Life in Its Origin and on the Dignity of Procreation: Replies to Certain Questions of the Day," February 22, 1987, www.vatican.va.

2. The Church has encouraged physicians and researchers to find ways to help infertile couples correct their infertility in moral ways. One person who has done so in a spectacular way is Dr. Tom Hilgers of the Pope Paul VI Institute in Omaha, Nebraska. He has refined what he calls "NaPro

Technology," a technology developed from an in-depth study of the female reproductive system.

3. Beach Center for Infertility, Endocrinology and IVF, www.beachcenter.com.

4. See Centers for Disease Control, www.cdc.gov.

5. See National Center for Policy Analysis, "Birth Defect Rate Higher With In Vitro Fertilization, October 31, 2002, www.ncpa.org.

6. *Donum Vitae*, II, A, 3.

7. Several good articles on both sides of the question can be found in *The National Catholic Bioethics Quarterly* 5:1 (Spring 2005).

8. Pope Pius XII, "Address to Midwives on the Nature of Their Profession," October 29, 1951, www.catholicculture.org.

9. See "China Male-Female Ratio Worsening," www.euthanasia.com.

10. See Stephen Bozzo, "The Morality of Ovarian Transplants," *Ethics and Medics* 30:9 (September 2005).

Chapter Four: Contraception, Sterilization and Natural Family Planning

1. Janet E. Smith's talk "Contraception: Why Not?" covers these issues. A new and revised version is available at www.mycatholicfaith.org.

2. For a collection of historical Protestant statements against contraception, see Charles Provan, *The Bible and Birth Control* (Monongohela, Pa.: Zimmer, 1989).

3. A good summary article is Brad Wilcox, "The Facts of Life and Marriage," *Touchstone* (January /February 2005), www.touchstonemag.com. The most recent studies about these matters can be obtained from the Heritage

Foundation, www.heritage.org, and from the Center for
Disease Control and Prevention, www.cdc.gov.

4. David M. Buss, *The Evolution of Desire: Strategies of Human Mating*, revised edition (New York: Basic, 2003), p. 175.

5. Glenn T. Stanton's *Why Marriage Matters: Reasons to Believe in Marriage in Postmodern Society* (Mehasha, Wis.: Navpress, 1997) details many statistical studies indicating that cohabitation prior to marriage increases the likelihood of divorce.

6. Chris Kahlenborn, Francesmary Modugno, Douglas M. Potter, Walter B. Severs, "Oral Contraceptive Use as a Risk Factor for Premenopausal Breast Cancer: A Meta-analysis," *Mayo Clinic Proceedings* 81:10 (October 2006), pp. 1290–1302, www.mayoclinicproceedings.com. The National Cancer Institute also notes a link between oral contraceptives and the incidence of breast cancer, www.cancer.gov.

7. Lionel Tiger, *The Decline of Males: The First Look at an Unexpected New World for Men and Women* (New York: Golden, 1999), pp. 42–43. See also, "The Magic of Sexual Attraction," December 16, 1998, news.bbc.co.uk; "Can 'the Divorce Pill' Wreck Your Relationship?" February 11, 2005, www.nbc10.com.

8. Tiger, p. 36. See also "The Magic of Sexual Attraction."

9. The major NFP information providers are Couple to Couple League (www.ccli.org); Family of the Americas (www.familyplanning.net); Billings Ovulation Method (www.billings-centre.ab.ca); Pope Paul VI Institute (www.popepaulvi.com). Online courses are available at www.woomb.org and www.marquette.edu/nursing/NFP. These sites feature studies done on effectiveness and user satisfaction.

10. See Janet E. Smith, "The Moral Use of NFP," in *Why Humanae Vitae Was Right: A Reader*, Janet E. Smith, ed. (San Francisco: Ignatius, 1993).

11. For an analysis of the effectiveness of NFP, see Robert T.
     Kambic, "The Effectiveness of Natural Family Planning
     Methods for Birth Spacing: A Comprehensive Review,"
     Hopkins Population Center Papers on Population WP 99-07
     (October 1999), www.jhsph.edu. He states that contracep-
     tives used perfectly have less than a 3 percent failure rate,
     and NFP used perfectly has less than a 5 percent failure
     rate. These findings were confirmed by another study
     reported in *Scientific American* on March 26, 2007: "A new
     German study, however, has found that, when practiced
     correctly, a method of periodic abstinence known as the
     sympto-thermal method (STM) leads to an unintended
     pregnancy rate of only 0.6 percent annually. This rate is
     comparable with that of unintended pregnancies in women
     who use birth control pills, the most popular method of
     contraception in the U.S." See Christopher Mims, "Modified
     Rhythm Method Shown to Be as Effective as the Pill—But
     Who Has That Kind of Self-Control?" www.sciam.com.

12. See Fletcher Doyle, *Natural Family Planning Blessed Our
     Marriage: 19 True Stories.* (Cincinnati: Servant, 2006).

13. For years anecdotal evidence has pointed to a negligible
     divorce rate for users of NFP; professional studies are hard
     to come by. See Mercedes Arzu Wilson, "The Practice of
     Natural Family Planning Versus the Use of Artificial Birth
     Control: Family, Sexual and Moral Issues," *Catholic Social
     Science Review* 7 (2002), pp. 185–211,
     www.catholicsocialscientists.org.

14. See the United States Conference of Catholic Bishops,
     "Married Love and the Gift of Life" (2006),
     www.nccbuscc.org.

15. For a good exchange on this issue see Benedict Guevin and
     Martin Rhonheimer, "On the Use of Condoms to Prevent
     Acquired Immune Deficiency Syndrome," *National Catholic
     Bioethics Quarterly* 5:1 (Spring 2005), pp. 37–48; and Janet E.

Smith, "The Morality of Condom Use by HIV-Infected Spouses," *The Thomist* 70:1 (January 2006), pp. 27–69.

16. See Edward J. Bayer, *Rape Within Marriage: A Moral Analysis Delayed* (New York: University Press of America, 1985).

17. For an excellent presentation of the issues, see Sue Ellin Browder, "Dirty Little Secret: Why Condoms Will Never Stop AIDS in Africa," *Crisis,* June 2006, pp. 12–18.

18. For a secular view of this partial success story, see Harvard professor Edward C. Green's book *Rethinking AIDS Prevention: Learning from Successes in Developing Countries* (Westport, Conn.: Praeger, 2003), in which he argues that secular Western bias promotes condoms in Africa to fight AIDS, where in fact an emphasis on abstinence before marriage and fidelity within marriage is more effective.

19. See Pontifical Council for the Family, *Vademecum for Confessors Concerning Some Aspects of the Morality of Conjugal Life,* February 12, 1997, particularly section 13, www.vatican.va.

20. See United States Bishops Conference, "The Ethical and Religious Directives for Health Care Services," directive 36, www.usccb.org.

21. See Dr. and Mrs. J.C. Willke, *Why Can't We Love Them Both? Questions and Answers About Abortion* (Pittsburgh: Hayes, 2000), chapter 29.

22. Society for the Protection of Unborn Children, "Morning-After Pills and Other Abortifacients," www.spuc.org.uk.

23. David Reardon, "Twice Violated: The Abortion Experience for Victims of Rape and Incest," *Celebrate Life,* Fall 1990, pp. 12–15.

24. Catholic Medical Association Position Paper on HPV Immunization, January 18, 2007, www.cathmed.org.

25. For a discussion of the Vatican decision about nuns in the Congo, see Bayer, pp. 88–96.

26. Bayer, p. 69.

27. Congregation for the Doctrine of the Faith, "Responses to Questions Proposed Concerning 'Uterine Isolation' and Related Matters," July 1993, www.vatican.va.

28. See John L. Long, *Sterilization Reversal: A Generous Act of Love* (Dayton: One More Soul, 2003).

29. Long, p. 224.

Chapter Five: End-of-Life Issues

1. Congregation for the Doctrine of the Faith, *Declaration on Euthanasia,* section II, www.vatican.va.

2. Pope John Paul II, Encyclical Letter *Veritatis Splendor,* The Splendor of Truth, August 6, 1993 (Boston: St. Paul, 1993), pp. 65–66.

3. For a philosophical defense, see Patrick Lee, "Human Beings Are Animals," *Natural Law and Moral Inquiry: Ethics, Metaphysics, and Politics in the Work of Germain Grisez*, Robert P. George, ed. (Washington: Georgetown University Press, 1998), pp. 135–151.

4. Address of John Paul II to the International Congress on "Life-Sustaining Treatments and Vegetative State: Scientific Advances and Ethical Dilemmas," March 20, 2004, no. 3, www.vatican.va.

5. "Life-Sustaining Treatments and Vegetative State," no. 4.

6. "Life-Sustaining Treatments and Vegetative State," no. 6.

7. Philip R. Muskin, "The Request to Die: Role for a Psychodynamic Perspective on Physician-Assisted Suicide," *Journal of the American Medical Association* 279:4 (January 28, 1998), pp. 323–328.

8. A helpful organization is the International Task Force on Euthanasia, www.internationaltaskforce.org. Some dioceses and bishops' conferences provide sample advance directive forms. The Bishops Conference of New Jersey has a useful site: www.njcathconf.com.

9. D. Alan Shewmon, "Is It Reasonable to Use the UK Protocol for the Clinical Diagnosis of 'Brain Stem Death' as a Basis for Diagnosing Death?" in *Issues for a Catholic Bioethic: Proceedings of the International Conference to Celebrate the Twentieth Anniversary of the Foundation of the Linacre Centre, 28–31 July 1997,* Luke Gormally, ed. (London: Linacre Center, 1999), pp. 315–333.

10. Pope John Paul II, Address to the Eighteenth International Congress of the Transplantation Society, August 29, 2000, no. 5, www.vatican.va.

11. Address to the Congress of the Transplantation Society, no. 5, emphasis added.

12. See Greg Burke, "A Non-Heart-Beating Donor Protocol," *Ethics and Medics* 25: 4 (April 2000).

13. Nancy Valko, "Ethical Implications of Non-Heart-Beating Organ Donation," *Voices* 17:3 (Michaelmas 2002), www.wf-f.org.

14. Hilary White, "Andrea Clark Dies of Natural Causes: Family Grateful for Pro-life Intervention," May 6, 2006, Lifesitenews, www.lifesite.net.

Chapter Six: Cooperation With Evil

1. See Pontifical Academy for Life, "Moral Reflections on Vaccines Prepared From Cells Derived From Aborted Human Foetuses," June 9, 2005, www.cogforlife.org.

2. "Moral Reflections on Vaccines," p. 6.

3. For a defense of this parsing of the intention/foresight distinction, see Christopher Kaczor, *Proportionalism and the*

Natural Law Tradition (Washington: Catholic University of America Press, 2002), chap. 4.

4. For a thoughtful treatment of religious liberty, see Kevin Seamus Hasson, *The Right to Be Wrong: Ending the Culture War Over Religion in America* (San Francisco: Encounter, 2005).